Dr Ellie Nik is an educator, holding a PhD from the University of New South Wales in Sydney, Australia. Her dedication to education and learning is unparalleled, reflected in her role as an internationally certified Results Coach. Passionate about personal development, Dr Nik's journey has taken her across continents as she remains steadfast in her commitment to authenticity and self-discovery. Much like a Phoenix rising from the ashes, she embraces each challenge as an opportunity for rebirth, continually striving to unite with her higher self on her transformative journey.

To Cameron (Mehrbanam), an unwavering pillar of support
in my new life's journey.

Dr Ellie Nik

EVOLVE: THE JOURNEY OF A NEW ME

A Memoir and an Invitation to Inspiring Change

AUSTIN MACAULEY PUBLISHERS™

LONDON • CAMBRIDGE • NEW YORK • SHARJAH

A CIP catalogue record for this title is available from the British Library.

ISBN 9781035871070 (Paperback)
ISBN 9781035871087 (ePub e-book)

www.austinmacauley.com

First Published 2024
Austin Macauley Publishers Ltd®
1 Canada Square
Canary Wharf
London
E14 5AA

Table of Contents

Prologue
Ink and Inspiration

All sorrows can be borne if you put them into a story or tell a story about them.

— Karen Blixen

Don't die with your music still in you

— Wayne Dyer

In the depths of my heart, an ember of longing had smouldered for years—a fervent desire to transcribe the chronicles of my existence into a testament of not only survival but thriving, a beacon of hope for those treading a parallel path of healing and self-transformation. This book, this collection of ink and paper, emerges as a pivotal chapter in my own odyssey, a mirror reflecting the arduous journey of self-discovery and transcendence.

This book stands as a significant milestone, propelled by a profound motivation—to touch at least one person's life. If it resonates with one individual, making them feel less alone, and sparking the courage and the audacity to explore their full potential, I will consider it a success. Writing, for me, is therapeutic, a form of healing. In these pages, I have stitched together the threads of my healing journey, believing that writing helps us understand, reflect, and connect the dots of our experiences as the late Steve Jobs would say.

While this book propels me out of my comfort zone, realising a lifelong dream, it also embraces the unfamiliar. Despite penning various stories, articles, and academic works, this is the first time I am sharing my life's lessons, learnings, and experiences. It is a labour of love, dedicated particularly to women and girls navigating the constraints of limiting socialisation—a message of freedom and empowerment.

For fellow migrants, I offer my experiences as a source of connection, understanding, and inspiration. My wish is that this book motivates meaningful action in your lives. Return to these pages whenever you need guidance, inspiration, and love for your journeys at different junctures.

The compulsion to write is not mere catharsis; it is a deliberate act of introspection—a meticulous endeavour to unearth the buried gems of understanding. To string together the fragments of life, connecting them with the delicate threads of reason, is a pursuit that weaves the tapestry of my past, present, and future.

Hidden away in the recesses of my computer folders, interspersed amidst the tapestry of Facebook posts, Instagram snapshots and ink-scribbled notes lay remnants of this tale, patiently awaiting their moment. The whisper of destiny beckoned, and this year, like a fragile cocoon unfurling its wings, I sensed that it was finally time to unite these scattered musings and memories.

I recall the words of Louise Hay, reverberating in my mind like a mantra: 'Write the book. You might decide not to publish it. But you will not be the same person who started writing the book in the first place,' and let me tell you that I am definitely not the person who started writing this book. These words fuel my resolve, an unwavering flame, as I labour over each line and paragraph in this manuscript you now hold.

The cover, a luminous shade of yellow, mirrors the vivid hue of my visions each time I contemplated the creation of this book—a vision of it ascending the ranks to become a cherished bestseller, an image of me in conversation with the indomitable Oprah Winfrey. Oprah, an eternal source of inspiration since my discovery of her in an English reading book at the tender age of sixteen. "Wow!" I whispered to myself, captivated by her ascent against the odds. Her wisdom, her indomitable spirit, and her legendary interviews with luminaries from all walks of life have held me spellbound.

So, Oprah, here I stand, an aspiring author with a heart brimming with gratitude.

My aspiration for this book transcends mere words; it is a fervent plea that it is read with empathy rather than sympathy. I did not choose the land of my birth, but I did choose Australia as my cherished home—a country where I have stumbled, fallen, and risen again, a place where I have forged my identity.

As you, dear reader, embark upon this literary voyage, I extend my heartfelt gratitude. Your time, and your attention, are precious gifts. From an early age, I learned to cherish the profound significance of gratitude, appreciation and acknowledgments and so, with all my heart, I thank you— mercilessly, deeply, and in every language that can express it—for holding this book, for joining me on this expedition through life, and hope, for sharing in my journey of healing.

This book extends an invitation—to be resilient, to ascend, to wage war when necessary, and yet to discern the moments when surrender is the noblest path. It implores you to embrace change, to treasure the singular existence we have been gifted, to inhale love and exhale kindness, and, above all, to heal together. Within these pages lies a testament that our journeys are akin to threads weaving the grand tapestry of human existence and that each one of us carries battles concealed from the world's gaze.

In this book, I offer you a step-by-step guide to evolving yourself, accompanied by real-life examples drawn from my own journey. So, buckle up and welcome to the transformative ride.

Keep shining, dear reader, for within these words, you will find the courage to illuminate your own path.

– Dr Ellie Nik

My Life's Calling

In the grand symphony of existence, if we are to decipher our life's calling, mine resonates with the echoing refrain of inspiration. I have discovered this not through proclamations or manifestos but in the quiet interludes of life – in the jobs I have held, the conversations I have nurtured, and sometimes, even in the profound eloquence of silence, and more importantly, in my life's journey.

What is fascinating is that my very name, Ellie, embodies this essence. Born from the wellsprings of hope and aspiration, it is a moniker bestowed with intentions—and its meaning could not be more apt. My journey is an intriguing ode to this name, a testament to my enduring role as an inspiration in the lives of others.

With a heart that cradles the confidences of many, I have stood as a steadfast pillar of strength, guarding secrets that shall accompany me to the beyond. Through more than 15 years of teaching English to speakers of other languages, I have sown the seeds of inspiration in countless students. They lauded not just my teaching methods but also my outlook on life, drawing encouragement from my unyielding positivity.

In my roles as a researcher, a lecturer, and a tutor, my unwavering optimism has received accolades. As I reflect upon my journey, it is clear that despite altering my name[1], the essence of Ellie remains intact. It signifies a source beyond the ordinary—an inspiration that emanates from the depths of my being.

As I inscribe these words, I embark on a new chapter, poised to become a life coach and accompany people in their self-evolving. My purpose now is to walk beside individuals on their path to self-discovery, nurturing the best versions of themselves. I will be there to cheer them on, to hold their hands, and to be the unwavering source of inspiration they need.

This wellspring of inspiration may have flickered in certain phases of my life, obscured by personal challenges, but it has never been extinguished. Today, it shines brighter than ever. As you read these lines, I trust that you can feel the energy, the connection, and the empathy that courses through my words.

If life has a calling, mine is to be a wellspring of inspiration. Whether in the guise of a teacher, a friend, or a life coach, I embrace this calling with open arms. I could not be more content to embrace my responsibility and serve to the best of my abilities.

---

[1] I have changed my name from Elham to Ellie; yet both mean inspiration, light and coming from the above.

Chapter One
Life in Iran

Unveiling the Mosaic: From Childhood to Adolescence and Adulthood

In the heart of Tabriz, a city nestled amidst the undulating landscapes of East Azerbaijan, my life unfurled against a backdrop of snow-clad mountains and crisp, biting cold. This land, with its dramatic terrain, would come to symbolise not only my place of birth but also the arduous terrain of my life's journey.

Now, let's delve into my early childhood, which is a bit of an intricate tale. It all begins with a revelation my mother once shared, an inadvertent secret that would change my perspective forever. She confided that, in the grand design of our family, I was not exactly part of the original plan. You see, they had orchestrated the arrival of my elder brother a good year and a half before I made my entrance into the world. According to my mother, their decision was driven by a lack of knowledge about using contraception in our home country.

The story goes that one day, almost unexpectedly, she discovered she was pregnant with me. That unplanned moment, as I came to understand later in life, was the serendipitous twist of fate that brought me into existence. It is not the kind of detail you wish to learn about your birth, is it? I have always known that my mother loves me. Her actions and affections have never left any doubt in my mind. However, it is safe to say that telling a child they were an 'accident' is not the most reassuring choice of words. So, for any parents reading this, my humble suggestion would be to spare your child the knowledge of being an 'accident.'

But that is not where the twists in my birth story end. For the longest time, I believed that my birthday was the same as my brother's, just with the month, and day, all lining up neatly on the 6 July. However, in my teenage years, I uncovered the truth—my real birthday falls on the 29 July. The reason my mother gave for this discrepancy was something along the lines of her needing more time for maternity leave. So now, I have two birthdays, and 29 July became the day I usually celebrate, a dual celebration of sorts.

Birthday celebrations, or the lack thereof, hold another curious chapter of my childhood. Strangely enough, I do not have a single photograph from my early years that captures the essence of a birthday celebration. No cake, no pointy birthday hats—just me, and the everyday moments. It seems that birthday festivities were not a prominent feature in our household. Surprisingly, this lack of birthday merriment extended to my brother as well. I find it intriguing that, as children, we never experienced the jubilant rituals of birthday parties. There is not a single photograph to serve as a testament to these milestones.

In adulthood, I discovered the wonder of birthdays, as they became more than just the ticking of the calendar for me. There were joyous celebrations, parties, and the feeling of being cherished. However, when I look back on my childhood, I cannot recall a single instance of a birthday party. It is as though those early years had an invisible veil over them, concealing the birthday festivities that are so commonplace for many.

Adding to this enigma is the fact that my brother has numerous photographs from his infancy, capturing those tender moments of his early years. But as for me, a newborn's image is conspicuously absent from our family albums. Sure, there are photographs of my childhood—of me crawling, playing, and growing—but none from the very beginning, when I was a tiny, fragile being.

In the midst of these discoveries, a peculiar thought crossed my young mind—perhaps I was adopted. I vividly remember broaching the subject with my parents, their responses firmly dispelling my unwarranted doubts. I bear a resemblance to them, particularly to one of my paternal aunts, which is more apparent now. But as a child, blissfully lost in the world of my imagination, these pieces of information led me to entertain the notion that I might not be their biological child. After all, they had not been forthcoming with these truths.

So, that is the complex patchwork of my early years—the knowledge of being an 'accident,' the revelation of a different birth date, the absence of birthday parties, and the enigma surrounding my newborn photographs. It all combines to create a mix of emotions and memories from my childhood, a tale that is both unique and thought-provoking.

From the very genesis of my existence, life unveiled itself as an intricate tapestry woven with the threads of challenge and resilience. My parents, both educators, cultivated an environment where the tenets of knowledge were exalted to celestial heights. Within the walls of our home, an unwavering devotion to education was the guiding principle. To be educated, to excel in studies, to amass commendable marks—these were not just goals; they were the very foundation of virtue, the quintessential traits of a good child.

But the definition of a 'good girl' extended far beyond academic prowess. I was instilled with the art of coyness and shyness, and my voice, though vibrant and unbridled in childhood, was gently nudged towards silence. Dissent and disagreement, I was taught, were roads best avoided. Thus, I learned to nod and acquiesce, tiptoeing around the desires of my older brother, a figure almost two years my senior. In this delicate dance, I became the embodiment of a 'good girl,' held aloft on a pedestal of parental approval.

Blissfully ignorant of alternatives, I found contentment in fulfilling my parents' expectations, basking in the warmth of their smiles at my docility. Influenced by their values, I began to nurture aspirations of becoming a teacher, albeit one who would grace the esteemed halls of a university—a place of prestige and honour.

The contours of my childhood were etched with the indelible influence of my older brother, an intellectual beacon whose studiousness I ardently admired. My life's trajectory became singular and unswerving—education was my north star, and I pursued it with a singular focus. My journey was a one-way street, a path I would later come to question.

Religion, too, was an integral part of my upbringing. Fear was inculcated in me from the earliest days, as the spectre of hellfire loomed ever-present. The mere notion that straying from the path of righteousness could consign me to eternal flames haunted my thoughts. As I grew older, a peculiar dread took root—if a strand of my hair were to reveal itself, I would be suspended from it on Judgment Day, a terrifying notion drilled into me by Islamic religious instructors at school.

Avoiding interaction with boys became a sacred mandate, driven by a belief that purity was to be preserved at all costs. Iran, under the rule of Islamic law since the 1979 revolution, adhered rigorously to gender segregation in education. My early years in a village allowed for co-educational learning, but when my family moved to Tabriz while I was in grade three, single-sex education became the norm. It was a transition that marked the end of co-educational learning until university, where the sudden convergence of the sexes rattled the foundation of my life's experiences.

Many years of separation between the genders had created a chasm that now had to be bridged; a transformation as bewildering as it was unnatural. The pendulum had swung from enforced isolation to a bewildering coexistence; a shift that reshaped the landscape of my adolescence.

My entry into university marked a turning point. Determined to transform my life, I embarked on a strict diet regimen. Deep-seated body image issues had long haunted me, and I resolved to shed excess weight and reclaim my confidence. With the fervour of a zealot, I banished rice and bread from my diet, replacing them with contemplative walks that stretched long into the evening.

Within six months, my body underwent a profound metamorphosis, shedding pounds and rekindling my self-assurance. Empowered by my newfound confidence, I ventured into uncharted territory. Tighter uniforms (mantos) replaced conservative attire, my hair became a statement of liberation as I did not cover it all anymore, and long nails adorned with vibrant nail polish signified my blossoming individuality.

At eighteen, the prime of my youth, I stood at the precipice of co-educational spaces, intrigued by the allure of boys. Education remained a cornerstone of my identity, and it was only fitting that the first boy who captured my heart was a polyglot, a linguistic virtuoso, and an ardent bookworm.

Lacking the skill to approach him directly, I initiated clandestine conversations, eventually revealing my identity by mistake. Our first rendezvous was a scene straight from a romantic reverie—an elevated pedestrian crossing, where two souls would ascend separate staircases, destined to meet in the middle.

Yet fear held me in its icy grip, paralysing my ascent, and I retreated from the precipice of potential love. Our conversations grew sparse, and he, in frustration, labelled me an 'abominable poltroon.' If only I had possessed the wisdom to navigate those delicate emotions more gracefully. If only I had been equipped with relationship skills during my education years, rather than spending my time memorising Quranic verses and conjugating Arabic verbs.

Undaunted by this setback, my heart set its sights on a new object of affection—a classmate of extraordinary handsomeness. Another attempt and another ill-fated outcome. I was learning the complicated dance of courtship through trial and error.

In the quest for love and curiosity, I decided to venture into the nascent world of Yahoo chatrooms, a digital realm that held the promise of connection. It was within these virtual corridors that I stumbled upon a life-altering encounter—a meeting that would alter the course of my life forever.

As our digital exchanges unfurled, a new chapter of my journey began, one marked by excitement, new experiences, and later, hardships and heartbreaks. This mosaic of experiences would lay the foundation for the challenges and triumphs that lay ahead, revealing the complex nature of life, leading to my first marriage.

My First Marriage

In the labyrinth of the virtual world, I stumbled upon the man who would become my first husband. It is a tale I have rarely shared. Our story sprouted from a digital chatroom, evolving into clandestine meetings and covert dating escapades. While I navigated the shadows to keep our relationship discreet, he, blessed with a more open-minded family or perhaps the privilege of being a young man, operated with a certain freedom. In the web of secrecy, we got to know each other, starting a journey fraught with a kaleidoscope of experiences—love, laughter, and the inevitable trials that accompany any relationship.

Our union unfolded against the backdrop of stringent cultural norms, where the idea of openly having a boyfriend was a forbidden narrative. I was cast as the 'good girl,' a label that dictated my choices and dictated that such relationships were inconceivable. Yet, fuelled by youthful rebellion, I ventured into this forbidden realm, careful to shield my exploits from the watchful eyes of my parents. However, the clandestine nature of our affair couldn't withstand the prying eyes of the morality police.

In a park, where we were merely having a conversation, we were caught, apprehended, and ushered into a police station. The dreaded phone call to my father followed, revealing a secret that unfurled as a scandal in the conservative climate of Iran in 2007. To my father's horror, the accusation was severe—his daughter, conversing with a boy, equated to a grave transgression. Threats ensued, restrictions tightened, and my world shrank. My mother's disappointment manifested in physical reprimands, and my freedom bore the weight of their disapproval. A painful hiatus from my boyfriend ensued, lasting eight months.

Resuming the relationship brought its own set of challenges, but the pressure intensified—it was not enough to have a boyfriend; I was obligated to marry him. Despite my inner turmoil and the palpable wrongness of the path ahead, we marched forward with a wedding that seemed predestined. Reluctant parental consent became the backdrop of a union I knew was a misstep.

Two years became a relentless quest to free myself. I cast my net wide, seeking escape through PhD programs and scholarships worldwide. The lifeline came in the form of an acceptance email from Sydney, Australia, marking the end of my Iranian saga. The divorce, a culmination of my pursuit of education and freedom, marked the closing chapter on a marriage I had entered against my instincts. As I embraced my PhD dreams, the echoes of that tumultuous chapter lingered, shaping the woman I was becoming.

Now, let me delve into the dream I harboured for a PhD scholarship.

The Scholarship Dream

Within the confines of my loveless marriage, I found myself ensnared, a delicate bird with clipped wings yearning for freedom. The oppressive weight of tradition, like iron shackles, bound me to a life I no longer recognised. The relentless drumbeat of societal expectations threatened to extinguish the flickering embers of my dreams. In this stifling darkness, I clung to one flicker of hope—a glimmering beacon in the form of education.

My family, devout champions of knowledge, held education as the highest virtue. It was this unwavering faith that nourished the seeds of my aspirations, sparking a dream that would carry me through trials untold.

With the resolve of a warrior, I embarked on a quest for a scholarship—a lifeline that could ferry me from these treacherous shores to the land of opportunity. My search spanned continents, unfettered by borders or boundaries. I cast my net wide, like an intrepid fisherman, scouring the educational havens of England, Canada, Australia, and America, each beacon of hope shimmering in the distance. For two relentless years, I traversed a landscape fraught with challenges, hurdling over every obstacle in my path.

The journey was a gruelling odyssey, marked by an unyielding commitment to excellence. I faced countless IELTS[2] exams, etching my dedication into each meticulously crafted resume. The pursuit of scholars and mentors became a global expedition, my digital footsteps spanning the globe.

---

[2] International English Language Testing System. This is the recognised English proficiency test for anyone who wishes to study a course in an English-speaking country and English is not their first language.

I waded through an ocean of applications, each one a fragile vessel carrying the weight of my dreams, and I waited, oh, how I waited; the seconds stretching into eternity.

Every night, as I lay in the hushed embrace of my bedroom, I conjured a vivid tableau—a vision of the airport. Here, I saw myself standing on the precipice of a new beginning, leaving Iran behind forever. The customary scarf, a symbol of my confinement, remained absent, and I revelled in newfound liberation. It was a rebirth, a glimpse into the future I so fervently craved. This vision became my north star, a beacon that guided me through the darkest hours.

Each day bore witness to a relentless cycle, a pendulum that swung between hope and heartache. A crisp Monday morning dawned, its pale light filtering through my window, casting long shadows of uncertainty across my room. My body ached with the weight of anticipation as I summoned the strength to rise from my cocoon of doubt.

Outside, the world awoke, a symphony of birdsong that danced upon the morning breeze. I reached for my laptop, its frame trembling in my grasp, as if it, too, sensed the gravity of the moment. With fingers like fragile petals, I typed my Gmail address into the browser, a trembling prayer for a miracle.

The internet, a sluggish beast, seemed to conspire against me, each passing second an excruciating torment. Time unfurled like molasses, the suspense almost unbearable. And then, like an ethereal apparition, it appeared—the word 'Congratulations' emblazoned in the subject line of an email.

My breath hitched as I closed my eyes, seeking solace in the silence. I clung to the fragile thread of hope, a tremor coursing through my body. With trembling fingers, I summoned the courage to click on the email, and there it was—a shimmering offer of scholarship from the University of New South Wales, Sydney.

Reality blurred at the edges as emotions surged, overwhelming me. It had happened. I had won the scholarship, and in that singular moment, a new path unfurled before me, like a silk ribbon beckoning me forward. This opportunity held the power to reshape my destiny, to approach my parents from a different angle, and to plead for release from the chains of my loveless marriage.

Hope surged through my veins, a potent elixir of tears, laughter, and a dance of unbridled joy. My heart, a wild stallion, galloped at a frenetic pace, a testament to the seismic shift of this momentous occasion. In that exhilarating instant, I knew exactly whom to call first—my mother, the keeper of my dreams and confidante of my heart.

A Magical Meeting: The Light in My Dark Days

We all need someone to believe in us, to reveal the potential that we cannot see in ourselves—especially in our darkest days, in moments devoid of hope, where closed doors seem to surround us. We all need someone who believes in us unconditionally; a force that empowers us to conquer the world. In the midst of my struggles, searching relentlessly for a PhD scholarship and fighting to break free from my first marriage, I fortuitously encountered such a person. They became the guiding light in those dark days, a stroke of luck and privilege that illuminated my path.

In 2012, within the confines of a classroom discussion centred on the institution of marriage, a heavy sigh escaped my lips, and I reluctantly acknowledged my impending wedding scheduled just a month away. An undeniable shroud of melancholy descended upon me; a complex emotion I struggled to articulate. It stirred within me, a restless slumber that had suddenly awakened. After the class concluded, a text message from a student, now a cherished friend, brightened my dim days, 'Let your smile change the world, but do not let the world change your smile.' In those isolated, desolate moments, when I grappled with the sense that my thoughts were in a foreign tongue, this message emerged as a radiant beacon of hope. A smile graced my lips, and I felt an assurance that I was not alone; my voice had been heard, and in the distance, there were promises of better days, their outlines still blurry, yet undeniably present.

In time, my student extended an intriguing proposition: the chance to meet an enlightened soul, a dervish, who could provide the guidance I desperately sought. Initially cloaked in hesitation, I eventually relented. With the impending wedding looming on the horizon, the prospect of this encounter held an aura of mystique and uncertainty. It unfolded on a wintry night, the biting cold exacerbated by a blanket of snow and ice that adorned the earth. My student guided me to the unassuming shop of this enigmatic figure.

As I stepped into the quaint shop, I could not help but notice the few individuals within, engaged in heartfelt farewells. My gaze settled upon an elderly man, his flowing white hair framing his face, receding slightly in the centre but retaining a gracious length around his head. His eyes held a mysterious luminosity, an otherworldly radiance I had never encountered before. Despite the novelty of our encounter, an ineffable sense of familiarity enveloped us. He exuded a paternal wisdom, a reassuring presence—a precious rarity in a culture that cautioned against trusting individuals of the opposite gender.

With a warm, welcoming smile, he gestured towards an empty chair. I accepted the invitation, and we shared a poignant silence charged with unspoken understanding. Tears welled in my eyes, a manifestation of the emotions that swirled within. He seemed to intuit my inner turmoil and began, "Perceptions may paint you as selfish, but deep down, you are not." His words unleashed a torrent of tears, tracing wet paths down my cheeks. He continued with a knowing gaze, "In a distant past life, you were a noble lady, a gifted pianist, surrounded by devoted servants and an impenetrable shield of protection. In this life, your journey has taken a different course, but the essence of that noble lady endures within you. Deep reserves of untapped power lay dormant, awaiting discovery."

With a reassuring nod, he assured me that brighter days lay ahead, even though, at that moment, such a prospect felt distant and inscrutable. Our conversation lapsed into silence once more. As someone approached the shop, I reluctantly rose from my seat to take my leave, bidding the enigmatic figure a heartfelt farewell. His warm smile, the embodiment of reassurance, remained etched in my memory.

On my journey homeward, I soared through a kaleidoscope of emotions; my laughter and tears intertwined. The boundaries of time and space seemed to blur, and the once-chilled night now embraced me with a comforting warmth. Upon reaching home, I could not contain my elation—I danced, embraced my father more fervently than I ever had, and clung to my mother with a newfound intensity. Although I remained silent about the details of the encounter, I poured my heart into conveying my love and happiness to my family. Inside me, a fire had been kindled, a blazing inferno steadily growing in size and intensity. That night, that serendipitous meeting, stood as one of the most profound and transformative encounters of my life—a divine blessing, a testament to someone who unequivocally believed in me.

I would pay visits to my newfound mentor now and then, especially during moments of uncertainty, such as when I awaited responses from the scholarships I was applying for. These visits became a refuge during tough times, whether it was after a disagreement with my husband or when the weight of loneliness felt insurmountable. Despite the outward appearance of a comfortable life with all the basics in place—jobs, a house, a car—deep down, I was not happy. Sometimes, our meetings would be marked by silence, a sacred space where unspoken understanding prevailed. In those moments, my mentor would encourage me to take deep breaths, reminding me of the immense potential within me that often went unrecognised. He saw a noble lady in me, and his unwavering belief fuelled my determination to keep trying. He assured me that one day; I would break free from the shackles of the wrong path, embark on a new life, meet a great man and even have children.

During some visits, he would play his musical instrument without uttering a word. The notes resonated in the air, creating a profound connection between us. I would listen, absorb the music, and leave, carrying the melody in my heart. I consider myself incredibly fortunate to have crossed paths with such an enlightened soul, someone with whom I could share moments of silence that spoke volumes. In those moments, I felt understood and supported in a way that no one else around me could comprehend. Even after my immigration, I carry the memory of his love and support with me; a constant reminder that he still believes in my potential. This belief sustains me as I continue to fight, thrive, and evolve.

Chapter Two
Journey of Migration

Arriving Down Under

The sun had not yet fully stretched its golden arms across the Australian sky when I landed on its shores one early Thursday morning. It had been an exhausting journey, a gruelling trek spanning nearly 24 hours, punctuated by two wearying layovers. To fund this ambitious endeavour, I had liquidated my treasured jewellery collection—an investment strategy I had gleaned from my resourceful mother.

A week before my long-anticipated arrival, I had struck up a connection with an Iranian couple who had generously offered to be my welcoming committee at the airport. However, the script of my journey took an unexpected turn when I reached out to them using a fellow passenger's mobile phone since I hadn't yet acquired a SIM card. It became evident that fate had conspired to keep them from fulfilling their promise.

With patience and determination, I navigated the serpentine queues, checked off the customs formalities, and claimed my two suitcases. Stepping out of the airport, I was met with the invigorating embrace of the September morning air, which playfully tousled my hair. My countenance beamed with an ineffable mix of relief and excitement—I had achieved the improbable. In the span of just one miraculous week, I had managed to secure the return of my passport[3], liberate myself from a constricting marriage through divorce, and gain the precious gift of freedom.

As I revelled in this moment, my elation surged, and I could not resist documenting it with a selfie in front of the sliding airport doors. This digital keepsake was destined to be shared with my auntie; a momentous occasion marked by the prospect of accessing the internet.

With a neatly handwritten address tucked away in my pink pocket notebook, the same trusty notebook that had faithfully documented my preparations for this journey, I embarked on the next leg of my adventure. My belief in the Australian dream burned brightly, despite my relatively meagre knowledge of Australia, a country whose identity was shaped largely by a childhood memory of 'Skippy,' a kangaroo whose name had only gained significance following news of my scholarship.

In pursuit of transportation, I sought out a taxi, and the driver struck up a casual conversation. When asked about my occupation, I replied with a simple, "I'm a student." He kindly offered a piece of advice, suggesting that I take the bus instead due to its cost-effectiveness. Grateful for the insight, I followed his counsel and boarded the bus, making a mental note to request that the driver notify me when we arrived at Kensington—the destination specified on my agenda. Yet,

---

[3] My ex-husband had confiscated my passport during the divorce proceedings.

there seemed to be a lingering uncertainty in the air, as the driver repeatedly inquired whether the destination was Kingston, Kensington, or something altogether different. Perplexed, I decided to alight two stops earlier than planned—a revelation I would only come to understand later—lugging my unwieldy suitcases, each carrying remnants of my 28 years in Iran.

The address I clung to had materialised only a few days prior, courtesy of a friend connected to the Iranian couple I mentioned earlier. Despite the uncertainty that loomed, I persevered, doggedly asking passers-by for directions as I hauled my laden suitcases up two steep hills. My breath grew heavy, my heart raced, yet quitting was never an option. I pressed forward until I arrived at a nondescript sliding door.

Behind that door awaited Father John, who had been apprised of my imminent arrival. His warm embrace welcomed me, and he graciously led me to my room, a humble yet comforting space. He explained that the other amenities were communal, but this small room was to be my new sanctuary, my secure haven where I would begin authoring the next chapter of my life.

As I locked the door, exhausted and emotionally spent, I collapsed onto the solitary bed within. Sleep claimed me swiftly, wrapping me in its embrace—a deep slumber that felt akin to the profound repose of the dead.

Settling into Life Down Under

In the gradual unfolding of my life in Australia, each day brought me closer to a sense of belonging. Navigating the streets, understanding the layout of my university, familiarising myself with the faces in the dormitory nestled within the embrace of a grand church close to campus—it all became part of my assimilation into a new chapter, a rebirth in a land far from my past.

As the contours of my new life took shape, I embraced the opportunity to make connections. Part-time work at the language school not only added to my financial stability but also infused a sense of confidence. The PhD journey became more than an academic pursuit; it became a voyage of self-discovery and resilience. I dipped my toes into the realm of dating, encountering fleeting relationships and short-lived flings, each experience contributing to the mosaic of my evolving identity.

Then came a pivotal moment—a Facebook message that would alter the course of my life. Hesitant, yet curious, I sought my mother's advice, a departure from the clandestine nature of my past relationships. Her encouragement marked a shift in perspective, and on a Sunday evening in May 2016, I met Cameron, my now husband. Our initial encounter lacked the cinematic allure of love at first sight; it was a simple conversation, a suggestion to drive me back to my dorm.

In the unfolding chapters of our story, Cameron and I decided to give fate a chance. A gradual progression of phone calls, shared moments, and growing affection paved the way for a journey towards love. Two visits to Iran, introductions to families, and shared dreams led us to a pivotal decision. On 14 October 2017, surrounded by friends, we exchanged vows in a modest ceremony. The echoes of laughter, the rhythm of dance, the flavour of good food, and the warmth of shared glances marked the beginning of a new chapter, and my wedding day stands as one of the defining moments in the canvas of my life.

The Journey Continues

Reflecting on the journey with Cameron, my husband of eight years as of 2023, it seems as though we have shared a lifetime together. He has become my anchor, my safe haven, my life companion. The words of my enlightened mentor manifested into reality when I met Cameron, the right man for me. Since our marriage, we have not only loved each other but have also grown together. In February 2020, our lives were graced by the arrival of our daughter, Eleanora— a bundle of joy, a chatterbox, our precious little girl. The decision to embark on parenthood happened organically after I submitted my PhD thesis in April 2019.

Our journey into parenthood unfolded during a trip to Japan, where we logically decided to try for a child. Unlike the stereotypical dreamer, I hadn't always envisioned having kids. The realisation of my pregnancy came in June 2019, and by November, when I was seven months pregnant, my parents flew in for a visit. With the impending PhD graduation ceremony in December 2019, it was a joyous time for all of us. Their excitement and support were palpable as we eagerly anticipated the arrival of our little one. Eleanora made her entry in February 2020.

However, the joy of new parenthood faced an unexpected challenge—the onset of the COVID-19 pandemic. In April, my dad returned to Iran, leaving my mum with us. Due to the pandemic's uncertainties, we sought an extension for her visa, and she remained with us until October 2021. Having parental support as migrants brought immense joy and comfort. The difficult phase began when it was time for my mum to depart, especially with a newborn in the picture. Emotions ran high, and the weeks leading to my mum's departure were filled with tears and emotional turmoil. The day she left marked one of the most challenging moments of my life, and the subsequent period tested us in ways we had not anticipated.

Farewell's Tears

With a heavy heart, I cradled Eleanora in my arms; her delicate frame nestled against my chest. The room was dimly lit, casting long shadows that seemed to mirror the sombre mood. As I gazed down at her, my eyes brimmed with unshed tears, and I couldn't help but notice how her eyelashes cast delicate shadows on her round cheeks. The room was silent except for the soft hum of the ceiling fan, and the faint scent of lavender hung in the air.

Tears welled up in my eyes, and I felt their warm, salty trail as they traced a path down my cheeks and onto Eleanora's silky hair, like gentle raindrops on a serene night. She murmured my mother's name, her voice soft and innocent, tinged with curiosity and longing. I leaned down and whispered, "She's gone back home, sweetheart. But don't worry, she'll be back soon." Eleanora nodded her eyes; a mixture of acceptance and a lingering sadness that she was trying valiantly to conceal. It was there, in the depths of her big, soulful, dark brown eyes, a silent plea for reassurance and comfort.

In the days leading up to my mother's departure, I had been an emotional tempest, each day more tumultuous than the last. These past two days, Saturday—the day of her departure—and Sunday, the stark reality of her absence settling in, had been the hardest to bear. I found myself questioning the boundaries of physical distance, grappling with the sacrifices and the relentless ache of longing. What if this was our last time together? The uncertainty gnawed at me, and I couldn't hold back the flood of tears any longer.

As my sobs echoed in the quiet room, I allowed myself to reflect on the profound bond my mother and I shared. We had spent nearly two years living together, nurturing and raising Eleanora as a team. In her presence, my mother had effortlessly slipped into the role of a second mother, a nurturing presence that often made me question my own abilities. Her innate kindness was a source of perpetual wonder to me, a quality I had always admired and secretly aspired to emulate.

Amidst the emotional storm, I clung to the knowledge that my mother had arrived safely in Iran, a beacon of hope in these dark hours. Through swollen eyes, I managed to utter a few sentences when I finally connected with her. I knew, deep down, that I needed to summon my strength, to weather this separation with unwavering resolve.

And as I continued to pen these words, my commitment to resilience and fortitude remained steadfast, a silent promise to myself that I would endure the trials of this separation, no matter how challenging they may be.

My First Car Accident

The morning weighed heavily on both Eleanora and me; our emotions entangled in the complex web of my mother's recent departure. This newfound emotional turbulence manifested in Eleanora's behaviour; she resisted even the most minor changes to her routine, from the simple act of changing her diaper to the task of getting dressed. I empathised with her, or at least, I tried my best to fathom the depth of her emotions during this tumultuous period.

To provide support, I had chosen to sleep in Eleanora's room for several weeks leading up to my mother's departure. My intentions were twofold: to offer comfort during this difficult transition and to encourage her budding independence. It was a delicate balancing act, a reflection of my personality that often led me to navigate life's intricacies with a certain duality—a trait that I couldn't help but find humour in, even amidst the challenges.

As we embarked on our usual morning routine, Eleanora's music provided a soothing backdrop to our familiar journey. Our route took us from Friendship Street to Alexander Street, a path I had traversed countless times. I adhered to my customary safety checks—glancing right, left, and right once more before initiating the turn.

Yet, in the midst of that routine manoeuvre, an unsettling twist of fate materialised. Out of seemingly nowhere, another car appeared, cutting across my path with unexpected swiftness. The sudden intrusion of this vehicle into my field of vision sent a jolt of sheer panic coursing through my veins. It was a heart-stopping moment; one that left my emotions in disarray.

Tears welled up in my eyes, and I couldn't contain the rush of raw emotion that surged within me. In the midst of this turmoil, I turned my gaze to Eleanora, her small frame securely fastened in her seat. Miraculously, she seemed unharmed, her innocence untouched by the near-encounter. A profound sense of relief washed over me, overshadowing my own shock and anxiety. It felt as though the mysterious car had evaporated into thin air, leaving us shaken but physically unscathed.

Summoning every ounce of composure I could muster, I steered the car towards a nearby bus stop, seeking a moment of respite to collect my thoughts. Eleanora bore a few stray tears on her cheeks, but her resilience shone through. As I stole a glance in my rear-view mirror, I noticed another vehicle parked on the opposite side of the street. It became evident that this second car was connected to the startling encounter.

Despite my best efforts to piece together the sequence of events, the memory remained elusive, shrouded in the fog of that shocking moment. What remained etched in my mind, however, was the sheer disbelief that the other car had seemingly materialised out of thin air—a heart-pounding reminder of the unpredictability of life's twists and turns, but also a poignant testament to our shared safety in the face of the unexpected.

Seeking Solace: Navigating Life's Challenges Through Therapy and Resilience

The seismic shift in my life that followed my mother's departure in October 2021, coupled with my first harrowing car accident, left me fundamentally altered. I suddenly found myself thrust into the demanding role of juggling a full-time job, the responsibilities of caring for a spirited toddler, the relentless demands of household chores, and the everyday challenges that come bundled with the immigrant experience. However, amidst this whirlwind of responsibilities, there was a conspicuous absence—a dearth of a close friend, someone whose unwavering support I could lean on. Regrettably, as I set these words down on paper, that void in my life remains largely unfilled. While I have cultivated friendships, there's an unshakeable longing for a connection that transcends the superficiality of casual acquaintanceship.

My husband, whom I cherish deeply, is also my best friend, and the bond we share is precious. Yet, there persisted a yearning, a subtle ache for something more, something distinct. I endured this state of emotional flux for an additional year, grappling with the mounting pressures and the tempest of emotions that threatened to engulf me. Finally, after mustering the courage, I took a significant step—a leap into the world of psychotherapy.

During a heartfelt conversation with my brother, he recounted a transformative experience he had undergone through Eye Movement Desensitisation and Reprocessing (EMDR) therapy—an experience that piqued my curiosity and ignited a spark within me. I longed to tread the path he had trodden, to confront my fear of driving and the pervasive anxiety that seemed to cast a shadow over various facets of my life. With newfound resolve, I approached my general practitioner (GP) and embarked on a course of therapy, with sessions meticulously scheduled for Fridays at 11 a.m.

My therapist, though initially exuding an air of formality and strictness during our early interactions, grew on me. Our conversations became a beacon of light in my week, and I eagerly anticipated each Friday's session. As we delved deeper into the therapeutic process, she broached the idea of employing EMDR to revisit the scene of my car accident—a pivotal step towards healing and closure. While I was willing to embrace this approach, I found myself grappling with an enigmatic resistance from within—an invisible barrier that seemed determined to shield me from confronting the haunting memory of that traumatic incident. Our attempts at EMDR therapy proved frustratingly futile, leaving me wrestling with a sense of unmet expectations and disillusionment.

We persisted with EMDR, exploring its application in relation to other incidents, but the results remained elusive. The profound and transformative experience my brother had so vividly described seemed to remain just beyond my reach, slipping through my grasp like grains of sand. While I continued to glean some measure of benefit from our therapy sessions, a creeping sense of futility began to cast a shadow over our efforts. It was against this backdrop that I made a pivotal decision—a hiatus from my therapy sessions, spurred by the belief that my mother's imminent visit would provide the solace and support I yearned for.

Looking back on this experience, I find a sense of contentment in my decision to embark on this therapeutic journey. It allowed me to delve deeper into the recesses of my own psyche, offering me a glimpse of self-discovery and personal growth. This newfound self-awareness became a stepping stone for my next significant decision—exploring the option of medication as part of my on-going path to healing and self-improvement.

Reunited with Mum: Finding Solace in Medication

The date etched in my memory, 1 May 2023, marked the return of my mother to Sydney—a day of immense relief and joyful reunion. The anticipation leading up to her arrival had been a form of therapy in itself. Her presence had been an invaluable source of support since the birth of Eleanora, and now, she was coming back to us. It meant that we would have family here in Sydney, a thought that filled me with happiness that transcended words.

In the weeks that followed her return, I found myself engaged in a candid conversation with my GP about the possibility of starting anti-anxiety medication. It was an acknowledgment of my need to rely on science to navigate the turbulent waters of my hyper-vigilance. My heightened awareness extended to even the smallest details—a piece of litter on the ground, a crack in the asphalt, or a hint of rudeness in someone's behaviour. These observations left me constantly on edge, whether I was behind the wheel as a driver or simply a passenger.

I booked an appointment and sat down with my GP, discussing the potential merits of medication as a way forward. One of my foremost concerns was the fear of weight gain; a side effect that loomed large in my mind. Body image issues had been a constant presence in my life, and at the time of writing this, I had cultivated a healthy lifestyle, complete with a balanced diet and sufficient physical activity.

My GP patiently explained that we could embark on a trial period, carefully monitoring how my body responded to the medication. It has now been nearly a month since I began this medication journey, and I find myself in a state of contentment. A close friend had once remarked, "I wish I had started earlier," and I could now fully appreciate the sentiment. While it may not be a perfect solution—few things in life are—I have noticed a tangible difference. The constant churn of overthinking, overanalysing, and obsessing over the minutiae of life has ebbed.

This decision to place my trust in science and grant myself a respite from the relentless cycle of mental agitation feels like a significant step forward. It's a recognition of the value of seeking help, of acknowledging one's vulnerabilities, and embracing the possibility of a more tranquil, balanced existence.

Chapter Three
Unlocking My Potential

In the saga of my resilience, my fight for self-discovery, and my journey of evolving myself, movement and music emerged as a pivotal force. Childhood memories are tainted with disdain for mandatory physical education classes, where sit-ups and forced runs were unwelcome norms. The imposition of physical activities left a bitter taste, and I distanced myself from the realm of movement.

However, as I entered university and embarked on my weight loss journey, my perspective on movement underwent a profound shift. I began to appreciate the importance and significance of exercise by walking and mountain climbing. The exploration expanded, leading me to the world of yoga, where I embraced the practice and became a dedicated yogi. Yoga became not just a physical activity but a source of mental and spiritual well-being.

Dance, too, played a transformative role in my life, embodying liberation and rebellion, a form of movement and art. Upon settling in Australia, I conquered another frontier by learning to swim; a skill previously elusive to me. In recent months, I have delved into the captivating world of aerial yoga, adding a new dimension to my movement repertoire.

This section of the book is an ode to these varied movements and my journey of learning to play the piano, each contributing uniquely to my journey of self-discovery and resilience.

Two Regrets, Two Joys

Life unfolds with its assortment of regrets and joys, two of which have accompanied me on this winding journey: music and exercise. The symphony of my existence carries these dual notes, one echoing with longing, the other resounding with fulfilment.

The first regret, like a bittersweet melody, is the resonance of music—the kind that is conjured by skilfully caressing the ivory keys of a piano. A lifelong yearning to create such a melody stirs within me, each note representing an unfulfilled dream.

I remember the longing gaze I would cast upon pianos in the shop windows; my fingers itching to dance on the keys. The allure of the instrument was irresistible, its ebony and ivory keys a portal to a world of expression. As a child, the world of music was tantalisingly out of reach. The early cadences of my existence were orchestrated around a singular note: academics. In those formative years, it was the pursuit of grades and marks that consumed my focus. The artistry of music remained beyond the threshold of my experience.

Physical exercise, the second regret, was ensnared in the tedium of school physical education classes. The teacher's insistence on running, sit-ups, and chin-ups left me with a distaste for structured physical activity. The air in the gymnasium felt stifling, and the drudgery of it all weighed heavily on my young shoulders.

My only reprieve came through crafting mini-projects that earned me passing grades, an oasis in a desert of disinterest. Beneath the façade of marks, the essence of why movement was vital eluded me, and the sheer joy of exercise remained undiscovered.

Cycling, a childhood delight was a freedom I cherished until societal norms wrestled it from my grasp as I grew older. The gendered restrictions on my choice of activities curtailed the simple pleasure of pedalling through life. A brief interlude with swimming came and went without leaving a ripple of lasting commitment.

Yet, the dawn of my twenties ushered in a rekindling of affinity for movement. The discovery of yoga was a revelation—a testament to the fact that exercise could be an act of self-care and an exploration of one's inner landscape.

The first time I stepped onto a yoga mat was an act of surrender; an invitation to unlearn the rigidity of life's expectations. The world of yoga unfolded before me, a delicate tapestry of poses and breath, each asana an artistic expression. It was a dance of the soul, a rhythmic conversation between body and spirit. The sweet surrender to Savasana at the end of a practice was akin to a lullaby, a moment of stillness that whispered the promise of renewal.

The yogic journey unveiled the beauty of synchronising breath with movement, a dance with the self that transcended the confines of PE classes. I discovered the profound joy of finding balance in postures and the serenity that accompanied the final meditation, a communion with my innermost self.

Migration marked a turning point. It was here, in the land down under, that exercise became a serious pursuit. Armed with knowledge and driven by a newfound appreciation for the intricate mechanics of the human body, I embarked on a journey of physical self-discovery. Exercise evolved from a mundane task into a celebration of vitality.

As for the piano, it was a dream deferred. The year 2018 breathed life into that dream when a piano found its way into my life as a birthday gift. It was an adult's awakening to the possibilities that had once eluded me as a child. Teaching myself to play, note by note, scale by scale, the melody of my heart began to take shape. Life's demands may intrude, but the piano remains a source of joy—a testament that it's never too late to embrace one's passions.

Regrets linger like echoes, but they are juxtaposed with the symphony of joy. In these regrets, I find the notes that make my journey unique, the desires that fuel my endeavours, and the knowledge that it is never too late to heed the siren call of unfulfilled dreams.

Mother Nature's Embrace: A Sanctuary of Solace

Amid the hustle and bustle of life, there is one place where I find an unparalleled sense of homecoming—nature. This connection with the natural world became an intrinsic part of my life while living in Iran, particularly in the northwest, where the landscape is adorned with majestic mountains. Mountain climbing, a pursuit I undertook in this rugged terrain, not only tested my physical endurance but also drew parallels to the challenges we face in our daily lives.

The act of scaling a mountain, I soon discovered, mirrored the journey of life itself. It demanded unwavering perseverance, akin to the determination required to confront the myriad tasks and obstacles life presents. In the quiet moments before dawn, as I contemplated the formidable task of rousing myself from the comfort of my bed at the ungodly hour of 5 a.m., my mind played the role of a cunning trickster. It whispered enticing excuses: 'Why should I leave the warmth of my cocoon? Wouldn't the allure of sleep be infinitely more inviting? The chill outside is daunting, and my body craves rest.' The list of justifications seemed endless.

However, it was precisely at this juncture that the true test of resilience began—a gentle but unwavering nudge to overcome resistance. I would summon the image of the ultimate reward that awaited at the summit—a panoramic vista that took one's breath away, accompanied by the comforting embrace of hot herbal tea infused with the essence of the mountains themselves.

With each sunrise, I triumphed over the inertia of slumber, most often on the blessed Friday mornings when the weekend beckoned in Iran. The drive to the mountain's base was accompanied by a burgeoning sense of elation and contentment, starkly contrasting with the notion of lost sleep. As we embarked on our ascent, we did so with unhurried steps, allowing us to relish the breathtaking beauty that unfolded before us. These journeys were rarely solitary; they were shared with cherished companions—my mother, father, or brother. On certain occasions, we ventured forth as part of a larger group, and it was during these moments that I couldn't help, but be struck by the camaraderie and warmth that seemed to define fellow mountaineers.

As we progressed further into the heart of the mountain, the path became steeper, and the air grew thinner, transforming each breath into a conscious act of willpower. It was at this juncture that negative thoughts sought to infiltrate our minds, like unwelcome shadows. Yet, I was blessed to have my father by my side, a master at dispelling these clouds of doubt. His words of encouragement, the melodies he coaxed from his musical repertoire, and the songs he sang became a symphony of support. It wasn't just my father; my fellow hikers, on various occasions, demonstrated remarkable kindness and encouragement. These memories are etched deep in my heart, a testament to the indomitable spirit of humanity and the bonds forged amidst the rugged terrain.

How I yearn for those days! Reaching the mountain's zenith was a culmination of physical and mental fortitude. The mountain breeze that greeted us, the warmth of herbal tea sipped from a flask, and the smiles of satisfaction that silently acknowledged our triumph—these were moments that transcended the ordinary. They were reminders, much like life's journey itself, of the lesson of perseverance. We embarked on each ascent with unwavering determination, progressing at a deliberate pace, pausing to rest when needed, and deriving pure joy from the journey itself. The summit was not an end; it marked the beginning of a new phase. The top of each mountain was merely a launching pad for the next adventure.

Through the art of mountain climbing, I found growth, I acquired wisdom, and I purified my soul. The absence of these experiences weighs heavily on me as I now reside in Australia. However, I remain ever grateful for the transformative power of Mother Nature, who has always been a steadfast healer in my life. From the serene strolls during my lunch breaks to exhilarating hiking escapades with friends in the Aboriginal lands of Australia, or even the simple act of sitting on a rock in silent meditation, it is all an embodiment of pure bliss. My heart overflows with gratitude for the awareness that has allowed me to discover the boundless abundance that resides within nature's embrace—a sanctuary of solace and rejuvenation.

Dance: The Rhythmic Rebellion

In the realm of movement, where the body transcends physical boundaries and the spirit finds liberation through music, there exists the profound art of dance. Growing up, I found myself restricted from dancing, primarily due to religious constraints that curtailed the joy of surrendering to music and expressing oneself through rhythmic movement.

I recall an incident my mother recounted, a time when she and her friends would gather to celebrate life, dance, and interact freely. However, my father's warning, driven by societal norms, put an end to those joyful gatherings. Dancing was deemed inappropriate for a young girl, and the rhythm of life was momentarily silenced.

Given the chance, I might have danced clandestinely as an act of quiet rebellion, a defiance of the norms that sought to stifle my spirit. Yet, it wasn't until my engagement party, my first marriage, that I boldly danced with both men and women present. While some relatives deemed it scandalous, I remained unapologetic. Interestingly, my ex-husband's family embraced a more open-minded perspective, which I sometimes find myself missing.

A confession lingers—a desire for closure with my ex-husband, an opportunity to bridge the past with the present. The yearning for resolution remains.

Post-divorce, I found my wings, free to dance whenever my heart desired. Dancing became a solace, an escape into pure expression. A significant step in my journey was when I enrolled in Azerbaijani dance classes, led by a renowned Azerbaijani icon. This experience reconnected me with my Azeri roots, expanded my social circle, and breathed new joy into my life. It even led to a performance at an Azerbaijani Nowruz party, pushing me beyond my comfort zone and further into personal growth.

Dance has played an integral role in human culture and civilisation since time immemorial. It has been a conduit for tradition, worship, celebration, unity, and even mourning. It resides within our very being, woven into the fabric of our existence. However, societal restrictions, ignorance, and bias have often suppressed this universal art form, especially for women. The oppressors fear the body and soul set free through dance, understanding that once unleashed, they cannot be imprisoned again.

In the midst of the on-going revolution in Iran, kindled by the death of Mahsa Amini, dance and music have become powerful forms of protest. Women are reclaiming their freedom by dancing openly, defying the constraints imposed upon them. Artists like Shervin are at the forefront, their music and dance embodying the spirit of revolution, offering a voice to the silenced.

Today, I dance to express my sadness, my happiness, my tears, and my laughter. With my daughter by my side, we leap and twirl, expressing our emotions through the language of movement. Dance is my voice, my solace, my rebellion, and my joy. It is an ode to the music that stirs my soul, a testament to the freedom I have discovered within its rhythmic embrace.

Yoga: The Journey Within

Stepping into that first yoga class, I was like an explorer setting foot on an undiscovered island. The studio's calm ambience beckoned me, and I clutched my yoga mat, water bottle, and towel, feeling a mix of anticipation and uncertainty. Simin, our instructor, embodied warmth and enthusiasm. Her infectious smile welcomed me into this new world, and it was there that my voyage truly began.

As I settled onto my mat, surrounded by strangers who would soon become companions on this journey, a sense of intrigue filled the room. What would unfold? The specifics of that inaugural class have softened with time, but the profound connection I felt remains vivid. It was as if yoga had whispered its secrets into my ear, inviting me into a graceful dance of movements, breath, and liberation from the ceaseless chatter of my mind.

Over a decade ago, a cherished friend—the same one who'd once reminded me not to let the world dim my smile—introduced me to this transformative practice. Their invitation was an entryway into a lifelong mentor: yoga, the union of life-force energy.

My journey has been graced by remarkable individuals whose names dance through my gratitude rituals. I send them waves of love and whisper wishes for their perpetual protection to the universe. Their presence continues to shape my path.

For me, yoga transcends the confines of mere exercise; it has evolved into a way of life. It is a lifeline I reach for when life's tempests threaten to unmoor me, a steady anchor that reconnects me with my breath, always within reach. Yoga, the art of uniting with one's true self, has unveiled layers of my being, revealing a treasure trove of potential that was always within reach, waiting to be unearthed.

Beyond the physical poses and contortions, yoga extends an invitation to step beyond the boundaries of comfort, to confront challenges head-on, and to explore the depths of oneself in each pose. It is a journey, an on-going odyssey, a pilgrimage into the soul. It is not about achieving perfect headstands or mastering poses with impeccable grace. Instead, it is about becoming fully present in every asana, about learning and growing with each breath, about diving ever deeper within, and about discovering the boundless potential residing there.

Through this practice, I have awakened to the truth that I am both the drop in the ocean and the ocean itself—a profound realisation that continues to shape my voyage. Yoga has become more than a physical practice; it is an ever-evolving journey of self-discovery, an on-going exploration of the heart of who I truly am. And again I say, a *journey* of who I am.

Becoming One with the Water: My Journey to Swimming

Swimming—a skill I never had the chance to master during my childhood. There were brief attempts as an adult, but I recall quitting each time, my ambitions quelled by the allure of instant results. Looking back, I wonder why I gave up so easily. The past is a realm we can't revisit, but in late 2022, I glanced at my bucket list, and there it was, etched in my own handwriting: 'Become a confident swimmer.'

Perhaps, for some, this may not seem like a dream. But for me, it was a profound aspiration. My childhood lacked the opportunity to acquire this vital skill, a life-defining ability, especially living in Sydney, Australia, a city adorned with beaches. They say that if one were to visit a different beach each day, it would take a lifetime to explore them all. So, my determination to learn to swim took root.

The last time I tried was around the age of 17 or 18. Regrettably, I quit then, though there were sporadic, half-hearted attempts in the years that followed. This time, as the winds of change swept the final months of 2022, I made a firm decision to realise this dream. I told myself that I would become the confident swimmer I yearned to be. I resolved not to waver or give in to doubt. In the spirit of unwavering determination, I enrolled in swimming classes, promising never to quit until I achieved my goal.

The stars aligned, and the suburb closest to us, the very place we now call home, welcomed adult learners seeking the art of swimming. This serendipitous convergence wasn't just a coincidence; it felt like destiny calling. It meant something more profound than mere chance. Notably, the new house we moved into had a pool. As I write these words, I can confidently glide through the water in our pool. It's not a journey without its challenges, but I am not a quitter. I press on.

The water is now my solace. Swimming isn't just a physical skill; it's my form of meditation. I toss plastic squids to the pool's depths, and with each stroke, I'm transported to a realm of serenity. I rise to the surface, inhaling the breath of life, and revel in the simple joy of floating on the water. I gaze up at the boundless skies, listening to the birds' melodies. I am overwhelmed with gratitude. This opportunity, this newfound confidence, this journey—I appreciate it all.

I am immensely proud of the awareness I have cultivated and the journey I have undertaken. In the water, I find peace, and in this new identity I have fashioned as a confident swimmer, I have found a source of pride. I visualised it, devised a plan, took inspired action, and now I can swim. I can glide through the water, a dancer of liquid realms. I can explore the depths, and I can simply meditate in the water's embrace. It is a feeling of liberation, and I cherish it.

Some might see this accomplishment as a challenge best suited for one's youth, but I hold a different perspective. The day I decided to learn was the youngest I would ever be. Time, after all, flows in a single direction. With this outlook, I seized the opportunity. I persisted and prevailed, and I couldn't be happier.

So, here I stand, on the shore of accomplishment, with my newfound love for swimming. The waters that once held my trepidation now offer me tranquillity and joy. The journey was arduous, but with each stroke, I have overcome not only the physical water but also the barriers within me. This is a testament to my determination, a reminder that age should never stand in the way of our dreams.

I took the plunge, and I can now proudly say that I have made waves in my life—a journey to cherish and share with anyone who dares to dream and take that first, resolute stroke towards their aspirations.

Aerial Yoga: Flying Towards Self-Discovery

For nearly a decade, yoga had been my sanctuary; a path to healing that transcended mere exercise. It had become ingrained in the very fabric of my existence, offering not just physical wellness but also a profound shift in perspective.

One day, as I idly scrolled through my neighbourhood's Facebook page, I stumbled upon an advertisement that piqued my curiosity. 'Green Yoga Studio' it read, adorned with lush greenery and verdant yoga silks. The serendipity of it all struck me—even the instructor's name was Green. It felt like a sign, a nudge from the universe.

On a crisp Tuesday evening in autumn, I made my way to that studio; my second venture into the world of aerial yoga. The first had been years ago, a fleeting encounter. I reminisced about that time when, unbeknownst to me, the seed of my daughter's existence had been planted during that class in May 2019. It felt like fate had circled back to offer me another chance, and I was determined to seize it.

Arriving at the studio, I carried with me the promise of an open mind, a mantra I'd gleaned from countless preparation videos. As I stepped in, my instructor greeted me warmly. I settled onto my mat, eyeing the vibrant green silk that hung nearby. I watched as my fellow yogis trickled in, each bearing their own hopes and aspirations.

Our practice commenced with the familiar rhythm of deep, cleansing breaths, grounding us in the present moment. Then, it was time to engage with the silks, to navigate uncharted territory. Every movement was a journey in itself, a dance between body and fabric. The novelty brought a continuous smile to my face, even as discomfort began to creep in.

The silk pressed against my skin, causing beads of sweat to form on my spine. The room grew hotter, the air thick with exertion. I kept pushing, battling through each pose, my hands working as makeshift fans. "I know," the instructor reassured us, acknowledging the shared discomfort.

In the midst of the challenge, a realisation dawned—this discomfort mirrored the struggles of life itself. Just as we chose the poses that stretched us in yoga, so too did we choose the challenges worth facing in life. It was about selecting the pains that would propel us into our growth zone, avoiding those that led to danger.

As the class wound down, we transitioned into familiar yoga poses, grounding ourselves in the essence of the practice. The final Savasana, a moment of deep relaxation, was like sipping from the wellspring of creative energy.

Emerging from that transformative session, I felt weightless, as if I could float on air. A smile of accomplishment graced my face, even as fatigue and a slight tremble took hold. The drive home was ethereal, the world outside bathed in a different light. It was as though I'd flown home, not driven.

In the quiet moments of reflection, I saw the profound parallels between enduring the discomfort of yoga poses and navigating life's challenges. Both required discernment—a choice to embrace the discomfort that led to growth, rather than the perilous unknown. "Your body knows," the instructor had said. Indeed, it was a lesson etched in sweat, silk, and newfound wisdom.

Chapter Four
Awakening the
Power of Awareness

In the pages of this book, if there's one powerful message I hope you carry with you, it is the transformational potential of awareness. This kind of awareness transcends mere recognition; it involves understanding and deciphering the threads of your life, the habits you hold, and the patterns you're entangled in. It's the moment you grasp that something in your life is not serving you well, the moment when you are confronted with a toxic presence, or when you sense the repetitiveness of undesirable circumstances. It's the 'aha' moment, the instant you awaken to the realisation.

For a practical illustration, think of a habit that has been your constant companion for years, one that has left you desiring change. The very instant you become aware that this habit is not a loyal friend but rather a thorn in your side, that is the moment when you can seek a new path. This is your cue to gather information, contemplate alternative habits, and seek advice from experts or those who have successfully navigated similar changes. This self-awareness is your launchpad for planning, action, and the first tiny steps towards crafting the new reality you desire.

Let me offer a glimpse into my own life to exemplify the profound impact of awareness. As shared earlier in this book, I have grappled with body image issues for as long as I can remember. I had repeatedly ventured into yo-yo diets without an inkling of why I consumed certain foods or their nutritional value. I lacked awareness about my own body and how it responds to changes. Not once did I consider the role of genetics, metabolism, muscle mass and fat percentage. My journey had been devoid of expertise, the guidance of successful mentors, or even the awareness to seek them out.

I remember vividly a period when I shed around 15 kilograms upon starting university. I was singularly focused on losing weight without contemplating the consequences of eliminating crucial nutrients from my diet, which ultimately led to hair loss. My approach lacked a long-term perspective; it was all about quick, immediate results.

However, the turning point was the awakening of my awareness, albeit gradual. I began to understand the profound relationship between our past experiences and memories and the food we consume. I embarked on a journey of learning, seeking knowledge, and making informed choices. My approach shifted from seeking rapid fixes to desiring lasting lifestyle changes. I took tiny, intentional steps, continually expanding my awareness and understanding of my body, my relationship with food, and the importance of conscious choices.

Today, my lifestyle is a testament to the transformative power of awareness. I consciously choose the foods I consume, knowing how they connect with my past and my memories. The knowledge I have gathered empowers me to decide what nourishes my body and what doesn't.

I will admit my life is not a continuous string of effortless successes. I still find myself occasionally drawn to foods that do not serve me or contribute to my well-being. But, as I always emphasise, life is a journey, a process. I am on the path of continuous improvement, constantly working to make better choices and grow as a person.

So, if you are to take one profound message from this book, let it be the potency of *awareness*. As the age-old adage wisely states, 'knowledge is power.'

Awareness & Acceptance: Unwrapping Life's Package

In the grand canvas of life, there is one thread that has had the power to reshape my entire existence—an intricate strand woven with the essence of awareness and acceptance. It is a thread that has gradually unfurled with the passage of time, revealing to me the intricacies of my own shortcomings, the complex dance of my upbringing, and the vast, imperfect world that surrounds us.

Imagine this thread as a magical ribbon that, when tugged gently, begins to unravel, exposing the inner workings of our existence. At its core is a profound understanding, a deep insight into the forces that have forged me into the person I am today.

It all begins with acknowledging the imprints of our past; the influences that have silently moulded us. For me, it meant peering into the very essence of my being and recognising the unique tapestry that shaped me—my parents, their knowledge, their limitations, and the environment in which they were brought up. This journey requires gazing into the mirror of our history, with all its glory and flaws, and embracing every facet of it.

This thread of consciousness has led me to a profound understanding of the forces that shaped me. I have come to realise that life is not a promise of easiness, but rather a complex amalgamation of hardship, heartache, and joy. It is a package deal, and the initial offering, like an unwrapped gift, is beyond our control.

In the mosaic of existence, the pieces are preordained— the place of your birth, the parents you inherit, the siblings who become your lifelong companions, and the legacy of your ancestors. These elements are the brushstrokes of destiny, painting the canvas of your life in hues you did not choose.

In my case, I was born in Tabriz, nestled in the embrace of East Azerbaijan, Iran's northwest region. My mother tongue, Azeri, is one of the many minority languages spoken in this diverse land. My parents, both educators, instilled a deep reverence for learning in our household.

I, however, was an unexpected arrival, a child born outside the blueprints of their plans. While my brother was the anticipated centrepiece, I entered the scene unannounced, an unplanned note in the symphony of their lives. To some, I might have been an 'accident,' but I choose to view myself as a blessed traveller, entrusted with a unique role to play in this world during my sojourn.

Acceptance means recognising that my upbringing was steeped in a particular religious context—Islam. In my formative years, this faith was followed without question, its practices etched into the rhythm of my life. As a girl, I was adorned with the hijab from my early school days, and my introduction to prayer and fasting commenced at the tender age of nine. Playing football or cycling through the streets was a freedom eclipsed by societal norms.

I do not assert agreement with these impositions, but I acknowledge that they were the threads in the way of my upbringing. They were the chords in the symphony of my early years, and to heal, I had to navigate the path of acceptance—to accept what was beyond my control.

Yet, as the years rolled by and I matured, a newfound awareness took root within me. I realised that I had the power to choose, to question, to challenge and to rebel. The structures that once confined me in Iran began to wane as I journeyed across continents. My awakening, my journey of awareness, began around my eighteenth birthday—an odyssey of self-discovery, empowerment, and self-determination.

This intricate mosaic of awareness and acceptance, woven with threads of acknowledgment and surrender, has been instrumental in my journey. It is a journey of understanding, of embracing the facets of my past, and of forging a path forward—an odyssey illuminated by the light of self-awareness and acceptance.

Knowledge Can Change You!

Knowledge, a powerful catalyst for change, carries the potential to reshape our lives and redefine our paths. The mere possession of knowledge, however, is not the crux of the matter; it is what you do with that knowledge that truly matters.

Think of knowledge as the key to an enigmatic treasure chest. You possess the key in your hand, but until you summon the courage to turn it, the treasures it guards remain concealed. Knowledge acts as the first step in the journey of transformation. Knowing about something is the initial spark, the awakening to the possibilities that lie within and around us. But this spark remains dormant until it is ignited by action.

Now, let's delve into this concept with a personal anecdote, featuring a man named John Kehoe. His teachings on mind power became an unexpected, yet serendipitous, entry into my life over a decade ago. I came across this through my brother by chance. At the time, I casually engaged with his mind power series. I dabbled in the exercises, glimpsed a hint of the potential results, and then life's obligations whisked me away.

But life is a curious journey, full of twists and turns. Fast forward eight years into my life in Sydney, Australia, and I found myself having an intriguing conversation with my brother. It was intriguing because it marked a notable shift in his disposition. For the better part of the past 15 years, most of our conversations were shrouded in pessimism and a sense of unease on his side. However, during this particular conversation, his enthusiasm was palpable. Something had changed within him.

Naturally, this piqued my curiosity. The spark of that initial encounter with Kehoe's teachings reignited within me. I resolved to revisit the source of this newfound knowledge. Armed with a fresh perspective, I delved back into the mind power series. This time, it was not a casual exploration; it was a committed journey. I listened, I took notes, and I diligently practised the exercises. With each revisit, I uncovered a deeper layer of understanding.

What makes this journey even more remarkable is how this knowledge harmoniously aligns with other philosophies, experiences, and people who have entered my life. It is as if all the disparate pieces of the puzzle are gradually falling into place, forming a coherent picture of my path and potential. And this book is a part of that puzzle.

But, let's not sugarcoat it; this journey is not a simple stroll in the park. I find myself juggling various aspects of life—work, family, self-improvement, nutrition, exercise, and more—all in my relentless pursuit to better understand myself and unlock my true potential. It is a formidable undertaking, but one filled with gratitude for the transformations it has brought.

This journey has underscored a profound truth: knowledge is a vital catalyst, but it is the action that breathes life into it. It is a continuous process, marked by both forward strides and occasional steps backward. What truly matters is your consistency, your unwavering perseverance, and your readiness to invest in your own growth. Steve Jobs once said, "You cannot connect the dots looking forward; you can only connect them looking backward." In hindsight, I see that consistency, taking even the smallest steps, and translating knowledge into action is the key to transformation.

So, let this be a reminder: Knowledge has the power to change you, provided that you dare to act upon it, if you remain consistent in your actions, and if you are deeply invested in your own journey of transformation.

Awareness in Different Aspects of Life

Throughout my life, I have encountered the profound concept of awareness through various activities, diverse readings, and poignant reminders. In the grand scheme of our human existence, two distinctive choices lay before us. We can either surrender, allowing the ingrained habits of our lives to define us, or we can boldly assume responsibility for the myriad aspects of our existence. Allow me to elucidate further through examples.

Consider, for instance, the practice of yoga, where even the most basic poses hold a wealth of transformative potential. Our experienced yoga instructor invites us to close our eyes and embark on a journey of self-discovery. It all starts with the seemingly simple act of standing. We are encouraged to delve deep into the nuances of our posture, unearthing profound insights into the subtle mechanics of our own bodies. Where does the weight predominantly reside, on the right leg, or the left, or perhaps it is distributed evenly between both? With keen attentiveness, we explore the curvature of our spine, distinguishing between slouching and standing tall.

At this moment, we are advised not to judge ourselves but merely observe. And then, the real magic happens—adjustments. With intention, we strive to stand erect, envisioning an imaginary line from the crown of our head to the base of our spine. Balance becomes our focus, an equilibrium achieved through equal distribution of weight on both legs. Through relentless practice and the continuous reinforcement of proper posture, we foster an intrinsic habit of standing tall, a habit that permeates our existence.

This seemingly straightforward example illustrates how an adult takes charge of their life. They embrace awareness, scrutinising their deeply ingrained habits. Seeking knowledge and expertise, they work tirelessly to enhance their habits. In the realm of a yoga class, they trust the accumulated wisdom of their instructor, honed over years of practice. With resolute determination, they refine their posture, ultimately achieving a superior posture in daily life. This revelation extends beyond physical alignment, influencing their emotional state, enhancing their mood, and generating a positive ripple effect.

This process of awakening and assuming responsibility is a journey, one that emanates from the moment we become aware that our existing habits no longer serve our higher purpose. Armed with expert knowledge, we relentlessly strive for improvement, harnessing the transformative power of awareness to amend ingrained behaviours. Awareness, akin to fire, possesses an innate ability to ignite profound changes. Once kindled in one aspect of our lives, it invariably spreads, transcending boundaries, and infiltrating various facets of our existence.

Embracing Transformation Beyond Weight Loss

While many fixate on the concept of losing weight, my focus shifts towards something broader and more impactful— a transformation in one's lifestyle. This transformation involves a multifaceted approach that delves into the nutritional, psychological, and habitual aspects of our relationship with food. It is about understanding why we eat what we eat, and why we tend to lean towards certain foods over others. For me, it is not merely about shedding a few kilograms; it is about initiating a profound shift in the way I lead my life, a change that transcends short-term goals and extends into a perpetual commitment to my overall well-being.

To elucidate, let me share my own personal journey. As a child and through my adolescent years, I was conditioned to associate food with love. Expressions of affection often took the form of enticing me to eat more, to savour another bite. This constant reinforcement ingrained in me the habit of indulging in food as an emblem of love.

However, as an adult, I began to feel the weight of this habit—quite literally. At the tender age of 25, I found myself struggling to perform everyday tasks; my breath growing heavy and laboured from even the slightest exertion. The time had come for a change, but my initial attempts at dieting were fleeting and unsuccessful. What became glaringly apparent was that a mere diet was not the answer; what was needed was a profound alteration in my lifestyle, one that I would adhere to for the long haul.

A lifestyle change encompasses a holistic transformation, one that touches every facet of our existence. It necessitates a deep dive into understanding our eating habits, our motivations, and our relationships with food. At this juncture, it is crucial to consult with experts, be it a nutritionist, a healthcare practitioner, or individuals who have embarked on a similar journey of transformation. These expert insights pave the way for a personalised, long-term plan, redefining how we view our existence in the grand scale of life.

Consider, for instance, starting from the vantage point of a future self. Visualise yourself at the ripe age of 90, exuding vitality and independence. Then, work backward, strategising the steps necessary to bridge the gap between your current state and this aspirational self. This approach is rooted in an understanding of your unique requirements based on your gender, height, current weight, and stage of development. Armed with this knowledge, you can decipher your eating patterns.

What sets this process in motion is a genuine desire to change—not merely to look a certain way but to feel lighter, more vibrant, and to love and respect oneself in a profound manner. The realisation dawns that this body, our lifelong companion, deserves the utmost care and consideration. It is, after all, the vessel that will carry us through the entirety of our existence.

Additionally, physical activity and movement play pivotal roles in this journey. Extensive research underscores the profound impact of exercise on our bodies, minds, and emotional well-being. Armed with the knowledge accumulated from experts in the field, we recognise the significance of regular physical activity. The choices are vast—walking, boxing, yoga, running, or any other form that resonates with our individual preferences. The key is to make an informed decision and incorporate movement into our daily routine.

Moreover, embarking on this transformative journey necessitates patience, starting small, and resisting the urge to overwhelm oneself. For example, in the initial week, focus solely on observing your portion sizes and select a smaller plate. This simple step paves the way for a gradual transition. In the following weeks, delve into the nutritional value of your meals, consulting expert advice and aligning it with your body's needs. Slowly integrate a 15-minute walk, three times a week. These small, manageable steps coalesce to form a profound shift towards a healthier, more conscious lifestyle.

Ultimately, the emphasis is on embracing a holistic transformation. Long-term goals prove to be more effective and sustainable than fleeting endeavours focused solely on losing weight. The crux of this lifestyle change revolves around feeling better, nurturing self-respect, and being acutely aware of the choices we make, not only for our bodies but for our overall well-being.

Mastering Your Thoughts

Now, let's journey deeper into the intricacies of transformation. Just as the position you hold on your yoga mat or the contents of your plate carry substantial implications, the thoughts that occupy your mind wield immense power over your existence. Consider this: What is the primary function of our minds? It is a seemingly straightforward query, and the answer is equally simple. Our minds, our consciousness, exist to think—to provide us with solutions, to generate ideas and responses, and ultimately, to guide us through the labyrinth of life.

In this realm, much like the aspects I have previously discussed, there are two avenues one can explore regarding the thoughts we harbour. The first path entails surrendering to the capricious nature of the mind, allowing it to meander haphazardly, absorbing any thought that may drift its way. From the daily news to social media, from past memories to future fears, our minds act like sponges, absorbing and regurgitating an unceasing barrage of ideas.

The alternative path, however, is one imbued with responsibility and mindfulness. It is the journey of active discernment and the conscious selection of thoughts that we permit to take up residence in our mental space. This path is not for the faint of heart, as it demands discipline, research, and consultation with experts. It is a time-consuming endeavour, one we are often unaccustomed to—but I assure you, the rewards are immeasurable. This is the path we must undertake if we aspire to change our lives, if we hold long-term aspirations in our hearts. It all begins with a deep commitment to taking responsibility for the thoughts that we entertain.

How do we embark upon this path of awareness and responsibility? We circle back to our grand plan, to the vision of our future self. What thoughts would best serve this aspirational version of you? These are the thoughts you must consciously allow into your mental sphere. It is essential to remember that this is not about force but about gentle transformation.

To illustrate, let me expand on this notion of observation. Throughout your day, at various junctures, take a moment to observe the thoughts that occupy your mind. For instance, you may find yourself entertaining notions of failure—what if you don't secure that job? What if you stumble and injure yourself during your jog? These are the 'what-ifs' that litter your mental landscape.

In these moments of observation, you hold the power to usher in transformation. Instead of waging war against these thoughts, merely replace them with gentler, more constructive alternatives. Picture yourself exercising with vigour, ensuring fitness and robust health into your 90s. This act of swapping a negative thought for a positive one instigates an instant shift in your mood. It is a delicate adjustment, performed without turmoil, and yet it bears the remarkable capacity to shape your mental landscape in a profound manner.

These examples, as simple as they may seem, epitomise the core of awareness in our lives. By grounding ourselves in these principles, we initiate change in various facets of our existence, from our posture to our eating habits to our thought processes. And, for each of these shifts, the fundamental tenets remain the same: observation, discernment, and a written purpose and plan.

In this journey of transformation, having a clear 'why' is paramount. When moments of doubt or lethargy attempt to thwart your progress your reason for initiating this transformation stands as your unwavering beacon. This 'why' fuels persistence, continuity, and perseverance, allowing you to connect every daily action to a grander purpose.

The formula is simple, my friend: Recognise the power of awareness in your life, and nurture it in each small step you take. Allow your every action to echo the symphony of your greater plan, leading you towards a future self that embodies the aspirations you hold in your heart.

Unlocking the Power of Language: A Journey into Linguistic Awareness

In my quest for knowledge and transformation, I embarked on a remarkable academic journey. I earned a Bachelor of Education in English Literature, followed by a master's degree in Teaching English to Speakers of Other Languages, also known as Teaching English as a Foreign

Language (TEFL). My educational odyssey culminated in the attainment of a PhD in Education. This academic foundation laid the path for my exploration into the world of linguistics.

Linguistics, the scientific study of language, has always held a special place in my heart. It is the art of deciphering the intricate web of words, phrases, and sentences that we weave to communicate, negotiate, persuade, and connect in our daily lives. As a polyglot, fluent in Azari, Farsi, and English, with a good grasp of French and Turkish, I have been uniquely positioned to delve deep into the nuances of language.

This intentional observation of language usage has been a fascinating journey. It is mesmerising how a single word or the arrangement of words can shape our messages and convey profound meanings. I have marvelled at the diversity of expression, how different individuals choose their words, dabble in terminologies, play with slang, or embrace the elegance of formal language.

I firmly believe that one's voyage of consciousness, self-awareness, and personal transformation can be greatly enriched by paying meticulous attention to the intricacies of language. It is in this exploration that we unlock the true power of words, transcending mere communication to connect on a deeper, more profound level. In this section, I invite you to join me on this enlightening journey into the captivating world of linguistic awareness, where the very essence of human connection is etched in the art of language.

Let me illustrate the power of language with a scenario many of us can relate to. Imagine you are in a doctor's waiting room, anticipating your 11 a.m. appointment. In the first scenario, you arrive five minutes before 11 a.m., and upon stating your name to the receptionist, you are met with a friendly, 'How are you? Take a seat; it won't be long.'

Now, consider the second scenario, where you arrive at the same time, greet the same receptionist, and announce your 11 a.m. appointment. This time, you are met with a different response: 'How are you? Take a seat. Thanks for your patience.'

These scenarios communicate the same essential message—you are here for your appointment, and you should take a seat while waiting to be called by the doctor. However, the linguistic effects of the specific words used in each scenario reveal a subtle yet significant distinction.

In the first scenario, the word 'long' stands out, and in some ways, may inadvertently provoke a sense of impatience. In the second scenario, the emphasis shifts to 'patience,' acknowledging and appreciating your patience as a client. Although the core message remains the same, the choice of words—specifically, 'long' and 'patience'—produces a different emotional impact.

This simple example highlights the importance of our choice of words or the tone we employ in our daily interactions. It underscores the significance of being mindful and intentional about the language we use in various situations. As we practice this awareness, it gradually becomes second nature, requiring less conscious effort and becoming an automated part of our communication habits.

I have observed these distinctions not only in English but also in other languages, especially Azeri and Farsi, where I am well-versed. In these languages, the choice of words and linguistic nuances can tangibly impact the message's effect on the receiver. Although I won't provide specific examples here,

I can share that these languages, similar to many others, often incorporate references to religion in everyday conversation.

For instance, in my mother tongue, Azeri, when discussing someone's endeavours or wishing them success in a particular task, it is common to use phrases that translate to 'God willing' or 'if God wants.' While these expressions carry a deep cultural and religious significance, they can inadvertently diminish the individual's agency and effort in achieving their goals. This is just one of several examples where language choices can significantly shape the message's meaning and impact.

Similarly, in the Farsi language, there are linguistic references to religious concepts that influence the way messages are conveyed. The notion of 'God willing' holds true in Farsi as well. Not using such expressions may result in a perception of not fully understanding the language or not adhering to the expected communication norms.

Challenging these linguistic conventions can be a delicate endeavour, as it touches on cultural and religious sensitivities. It is likely that other languages have their own unique linguistic nuances that influence communication. So, I encourage you to take a moment to reflect on the choice of words and expressions in your own language that might have different impacts on people, and how cultural and linguistic context can shape our understanding of messages.

Now, let's transition back to the English language and draw a connection between the concept of linguistic awareness and our internal dialogues as human beings. Each day, we engage in numerous conversations within ourselves, comprising various forms of self-criticism, self-praise, worries, fears, and diverse interactions with our own thoughts.

All of these inner dialogues fall under the category of conversations we constantly have with ourselves.

The nature of these internal dialogues is significantly influenced by the language we use and the automatic thought patterns we have become accustomed to, often shaped by our socialisation and experiences. Additionally, these inner dialogues are intimately intertwined with our self-image and our perception of our abilities, competence, and worth in various aspects of life.

If we are honest with ourselves, we will find that a substantial portion of our inner dialogues tends to be negative in nature. More often than not, we emerge as our harshest critics. For instance, recall your school days when you received a C minus on a math assignment. What immediately ran through your internal dialogue? Chances are, you thought, 'I'm really bad at math,' 'I knew it,' 'I'll never improve in math,' or 'I always mess up my exams.' These self-judgments and negative inner dialogues are a common occurrence.

Now, picture yourself as a tomato plant in a garden. It is your first time producing tomatoes, and the gardener notices that there are no tomatoes on your branches, while the other tomato plants around you bear a few. Would the gardener respond by scolding you, accusing you of inadequacy, laziness, or comparing you to the other plants? Some gardeners might react this way, but an attentive gardener would take a different approach. They would investigate the reasons behind the lack of tomatoes on your branches and provide the necessary care, such as fertilisers, water, or more sunlight, with the hope that you would eventually bear fruit.

This analogy illustrates how we cannot expect ourselves to thrive and flourish while simultaneously bombarding our minds with negative inner dialogues. It underscores the significance of linguistic awareness not only in our conversations and interactions with others but, more importantly, in the kind of conversations and internal dialogues we engage in with ourselves. It emphasises the importance of the quality of the conversations we have within our own minds and the profound impact they can have on our overall well-being and personal growth.

For those of us committed to the path of self-improvement and self-transformation, a critical responsibility lies in examining the internal dialogues we engage in with ourselves. This entails a conscious and intentional effort to filter and refine the quality of these conversations. Moreover, it demands an essential act of kindness towards ourselves.

It is important to clarify that this does not mean resorting to self-deception or falsehoods. Instead, it begins with the fundamental step of observing the nature of our daily internal dialogues. Once we have taken this initial step, the pivotal question to ask is whether these internal dialogues, in our newfound state of awareness, serve us on our current journey and align with the future version of ourselves that we aspire to become. If the answer is affirmative, then by all means, continue nurturing those internal dialogues. However, if they do not serve our current purpose, it is time to delve deeper.

We need to explore why we harbour these specific internal dialogues. Is it a result of conditioning from our parents, society, or educational upbringing? Or is it genuinely our own conscious choice? If we discover that some of these dialogues are not of our conscious choosing, we must endeavour to introduce new dialogues or replace the existing ones, just as we would with any other habit in our lives.

This process strongly parallels the transformation of various habits we hold, such as the foods we consume or the thoughts we allow to permeate our minds. Therefore, linguistic awareness, in the context of our internal dialogues, and our active awareness and control of it, is a monumental step in the journey of life transformation and self-development. Every individual must assume responsibility for this aspect of their lives because the nature of our internal dialogue profoundly influences every facet of our existence.

Our internal dialogue significantly shapes our self-image, defining who we believe ourselves to be and the qualities we believe we possess or lack. In essence, it holds the power to influence the entirety of our lives, making it a domain that warrants our utmost attention and care in our pursuit of personal growth and transformation.

It is imperative to set aside time each day at different intervals to pause and observe the nature of your internal dialogues in various situations. Take a moment to jot down these dialogues, keeping a record of them. Over the course of a few weeks, review your notes and look for any recurring patterns or themes that emerge.

If you detect patterns that do not serve your current journey and future aspirations, treat these patterns just as you would habits that need adjustment. Consider whether new internal dialogues are needed, or if some need replacement or removal. Reflect on the action steps required to nurture a more nourishing, thriving, and productive set of internal dialogues that align with and support you in your day-to-day life as well as in your journey towards your envisioned future self.

Acceptance

In the profound journey of healing, awareness and transformation there exists a pivotal chapter—the chapter of acceptance. It is within this realm that I first acknowledged my ignorance and took the courageous step of accepting it. As I recount my path to healing, I'm reminded that I have yet to reach a final destination, if indeed such a place exists.

I accepted the absence of vital social skills, those untaught chapters in the book of human interaction. The skills needed to approach a potential partner were a mystery to me, untouched by the education system or my upbringing. It's not a matter of blame, but rather an understanding that certain knowledge was absent. I embarked on a quest for comprehension and self-forgiveness.

Equally, I accepted my lack of knowledge about how to exit a marriage gracefully. The geographic confines I found myself in bestowed unnecessary privileges upon men while denying women their rightful share. My culture stigmatised divorce, particularly for women, making the pursuit of freedom an arduous battle. Many factors lay beyond my control, and my decisions were shaped by the unpredictable course of fate. Hindsight grants me clarity, but amid the turmoil and uncertainty, I was a passenger in my own life.

Nutrition, weight management, genetics, and the science of exercise were uncharted territories for me. I acknowledged my ignorance regarding the complex interplay of these factors. My culture's obsession with body image imposed weighty expectations upon me, where comments on my appearance became the norm. I felt compelled to react to every gain or loss, even though I had little understanding of the dynamics involved. I cycled through ineffective diets, met with disappointment, and was left perplexed.

The process of understanding why things unfolded as they did, and the acceptance of my past ignorance, has lightened the burdens of my experiences. Admitting to my lack of knowledge remains a challenge, but unravelling the threads of what happened and why has proven immensely valuable. In this on-going journey of healing, acceptance is the beacon that guides me towards self-compassion and enlightenment.

One facet of acceptance involves recognising that various educational systems have influenced our perspectives in certain ways. Allow me to elaborate on this.

The Education System's Unseen Faults

Education, the bedrock of society, shapes young minds and sets the stage for a lifelong journey. Yet, it is a curious paradox that within the hallowed halls of academia, there are deep crevices left unexplored.

Welcome to a world where traditional education reigns, but crucial life lessons remain unspoken. Our formal education, even in the most advanced first-world countries, often leaves students unequipped for the formidable challenges of life. This chapter is a revelation, a call to action, and an illumination of the pathways less travelled. It is about recognising the untapped reservoir of potential within us and uncovering the means to harness it, to channel it in extraordinary ways.

At various crossroads in my life, I could not help but wonder: Why does our education system omit the profound art of living? When and how, I wondered, do we introduce young minds to the profound significance of gratitude? Shouldn't our education teach us that we are not merely slaves to the thoughts we think, but powerful creators of our reality? Why does the curriculum remain silent about the rules of the game in this world, the unwritten laws that govern our existence? Isn't it high time we learned that we can not only follow these rules, but also rewrite them, moulding the world to our vision?

The intrigue of lifelong learning has long been my companion, an enduring passion. It beckoned me to tread beyond the boundaries of formal education, pushing the envelope of my understanding. To me, the cessation of learning equates to a stifled existence; the quest for knowledge is synonymous with vitality. It was the relentless pursuit of self-improvement, the unquenchable thirst for awareness, and the determination to transmute knowledge into action that fired the crucible of my journey.

Here, in 2023, a new chapter begins, and with it, a profound declaration: the mantle of a life coach. The curtain rises, and the world witnesses an unconventional odyssey unfold, dedicated to disseminating knowledge and awareness, nurturing the ember of action. The path before me is set, and my mission is clear: to guide individuals on a transformative journey of lifelong learning, a journey where knowledge, once unlocked, is the key to not just existence but an extraordinary, meaningful life.

One of life's most profound truths is the depth of understanding we gain as we journey through its various stages. It is a journey marked by ever-deepening layers of comprehension, where we revisit familiar subjects with fresh eyes and newfound wisdom.

Picture this: you pick up a cherished book from your bookshelf. It is a book you have read many times before, each reading unveiling new layers of its brilliance. Much like life itself, you discover that knowledge, too, unfolds in its entirety only through the passage of time.

Lifelong learning, a concept that has been my guiding star, has etched a multifaceted story of my own transformation. But it was only recently, in the crucible of this year, that I decided to chart a definite course towards becoming a life coach. This pivotal decision was more than a leap; it was a pledge to embark on a journey propelled by credible sources and a deep sense of pride.

Life coaching, unlike many professions, lacks rigid regulation. Anyone can lay claim to the title of a life coach, but I yearned for something more. I yearned for an education that bore the stamp of credibility, one that aligned seamlessly with my passion for lifelong learning. Hence, my decision to couple formal education with the wisdom garnered from countless books and the invaluable insights of fellow travellers along the path of self-discovery.

Formal education undoubtedly offers vital building blocks, but for every adult, it carries an inherent responsibility. This responsibility is to seize the reins of one's self-development journey, to curate the knowledge that will pave the way for one's career, and, most significantly, one's life voyage.

My formal education in the realm of coaching is but one facet of this grand quest. The pursuit of knowledge extends to the art of empathetic communication, to honing the skills of attentive listening, and to the art of walking alongside individuals on their transformative journeys. It is the inner capabilities, often dormant or obscured by the hustle and bustle of life, that hold the potential for remarkable achievements.

Within each of us lies the potential to conquer our goals, and sometimes, all it takes is someone to awaken those latent abilities. This is where mentorship and coaching take centre stage. It is in this role, as a guiding light, that I aspire to partner with individuals. I aim to help them recognise their unique potential, to traverse the path towards becoming their best selves, and to unlock their inner power.

The whispers within me affirm that this path, the path of awakening human potential and guiding lives towards transformation, is the path I am destined to walk. It is a journey marked by knowledge, wisdom, empathy, and the unshakeable belief in the remarkable capabilities that reside within each of us.

In assuming the responsibility for my self-education, I have found solace and guidance through my silent companions—books!

Books

Books, the silent knowledge-holders and the best of friends, play an indispensable role in our journey of awakening. They've been my guiding lights, my refuge, and my solace. From the very moment I cracked open the pages of *The Five Major Pieces to the Life Puzzle* by Jim Rohn, my love affair with reading blossomed. That fateful night, I devoured its wisdom cover to cover, and it felt like discovering a treasure chest of knowledge.

As the years passed, my hunger for knowledge grew. I embarked on journeys through pages, diving into *The Seven Habits of Highly Effective People* and countless others. Libraries and bookstores became my sanctuaries, places where I could lose myself in the boundless realms of human thought. I found solace in the hushed corners, surrounded by colourful stationery, where I could scribble my own musings and dreams.

For me, heaven would surely be a place overflowing with books, stationery, and the aroma of freshly brewed coffee. These companions have moulded my identity. When James Clear, in *Atomic Habits*, emphasised the importance of integrating habits into one's identity, I took it to heart. I proudly wear the badge of a reader.

That sacred hour before bedtime, where I lose myself within the pages has become my me-time, my sacred ritual. It's an investment in my personal growth, a doorway to new horizons. I have yet to embrace audiobooks or Kindles fully; the tangible feel of a physical book, its distinct scent, and the joy of flipping its pages remain unmatched.

Oh, books, my cherished companions, I am eternally grateful for your presence in my life. You've illuminated my path, expanded my horizons, and filled my world with endless possibilities.

The Calling, Ripe and Resolute

I must emphasise, that this calling, this unshakeable sense of purpose, has resonated within me at various junctures of my life. But it was not until now, until this precise moment in my life, that I felt it had truly ripened, ready for the plucking.

Just like a fruit that refuses to yield its sweetness until the timing is perfect, my journey into the realm of coaching was waiting for me to be at the pinnacle of my transformation. It demanded that my body, spirit, and mind be in perfect alignment.

This calling had been awaiting the precise life stage, akin to a flower patiently biding its time to unfurl its petals in full splendour, at precisely the right moment. I can feel it resonate in every fibre of my being, resonating in my mind, my heart, my body, and my soul. This, unequivocally, is the right time.

As I stand at the crossroads, I can sense the convergence of lives intersecting with mine. Lives that are ready, poised for the changes they have long contemplated. They are prepared to make a commitment, not just any commitment, but a wholehearted one. They are ready for the comprehensive transformation they have been yearning for, both in their minds and their bodies. They are willing to commit financially, spiritually, and above all, mentally.

The people I aim to walk alongside are those prepared to give it their all, forge a detailed plan, and possess unwavering determination. They are willing to embrace consistency and persevere through every trial until the glorious moment when their future selves materialise. I am ready to guide them through this transformative journey, equipped to lead them to the revelation of their future selves, step by step. I am prepared to meet the future selves they envision.

Their dedication, their unrelenting willpower, and their resolve to be consistent are what fuel my fervour. I can already envision the enthusiasm, the elation, and the exhilaration as each one realises their cherished goals. The sheer prospect of sharing in these victories, of achieving greatness together with them, ignites my passion and propels me on this very journey.

I sense that this is not just my path; it is my destiny. My skills, my knowledge, and my fervent love for what I do, all converge and align on this profound journey. It is my privilege to walk hand in hand with every person I encounter on this path. Together, we shall embark on this transformative adventure and emerge victorious, cheering at every milestone. Our achievements will be woven into the tapestry of shared victories. Hallelujah.

Chapter Five
Steps to Evolving Yourself

In this section, I will provide you with a practical, step-by-step guide drawn from my lived experiences, research, readings, and insights. It is a roadmap on how to evolve yourself, initiate the journey of self-transformation, and begin moving towards the best version of yourself that you envision.

Start with Why: The Transformational Power of Self-Love

The initial step in the process of evolving the self is to introspect and ask, 'Why do I want to embark on this journey? Why do I aspire to become a new version of myself? Why is change important to me?' One compelling answer to these questions is rooted in self-love, self-respect, and the inherent belief that you deserve to unfold into a greater, more evolved version of yourself.

Self-love is a profoundly significant concept, one that I personally did not fully grasp during my upbringing. However, I have come to realise the immense importance and impact it can have on an individual's life. Growing up, I was often told that taking time for self-care and indulging in personal well-being was akin to selfishness. In hindsight, I regret internalising such a misconception. It is paramount for every individual, right from childhood, to learn the vital lesson of self-love and to distinguish it from selfishness. Self-love is not selfishness. As I reflect on this, I define self-love as the practice of knowing and valuing oneself, dedicating time to physical, mental, and spiritual well-being in a manner that acknowledges our inherent worth. To make this a reality, it is imperative that we consciously allocate time for self-love and prioritise it as we see fit. First and foremost, it is crucial to understand the concept of self-love and differentiate it from selfishness. Teaching ourselves and society that self-love and selfishness are distinct is an essential part of the process. We must embrace the importance of loving and respecting ourselves, making space and time for our personal growth. I cannot emphasise enough how profoundly transformative self-love is, and I firmly believe that it encompasses self-respect within its core.

Furthermore, I would like to provide some examples to illustrate this point. Let's consider a situation where you recently realised that the romantic relationship you are in no longer serves you. While this could apply to any kind of relationship, I will focus on the context of a romantic relationship. There are often clear signs that emerge when we come to the realisation that our romantic relationship is no longer productive, aligned with our personal goals, or healthy for our well-being.

It is common for us to initially overlook these signs, reminiscing about the love that once existed in the relationship, the fond memories, and the substantial investments we have made. We might find ourselves making various excuses to justify staying in a toxic or unproductive relationship. This is where the concepts of self-love and self-respect become paramount.

For those who have been instilled with these values from childhood or have adopted them through self-discovery and personal growth, they serve as a guiding light in such moments of crisis. Self-love and self-respect come to the rescue, allowing individuals to make the tough but necessary decisions for their own well-being.

Of course, the situation becomes more manageable when both partners are understanding, self-aware, and willing to engage in open, honest conversations about their feelings and the signs they have observed in the relationship. In such cases, it is an opportunity to discuss these feelings with your partner, sharing the signs you have noticed. If both individuals are committed to the relationship, they can work together to address issues, provide mutual support, and potentially strengthen their bond as a result.

However, should you find that, during these crucial conversations with your partner, they respond by making excuses or shifting blame onto you, insisting that everything in the relationship is flawless and the problem lies with you, it is yet another clear sign that this relationship is no longer in alignment with your vision for yourself. It is at this point that the concepts of self-love and self-respect need to take centre stage. You must take the next step by having a serious and direct conversation with your romantic partner. Communicate your efforts to address issues and express that, despite your attempts, you feel that the relationship is not working for you.

Two scenarios might unfold at this juncture. In scenario one, your partner persists in blaming you and refuses to accept responsibility, which makes it clearer that it is time to move on. Scenario two involves a change in your partner's approach, where they acknowledge the issues and offer solutions to work on the relationship. In this case, you face a decision: whether to give the relationship another chance or not. What remains paramount in both scenarios is the unwavering importance of self-love and self-respect.

It is worth emphasising that individuals with a strong sense of self-love and self-respect are more likely to enter relationships with partners who share these values and are equally committed to investing in the relationship. This minimises the need to contemplate leaving the relationship. Nevertheless, life is not always rosy, and human beings are prone to making mistakes. Even if a relationship begins with love and harmony, people evolve and transform at different rates, speeds, and depths. Consequently, two individuals who initially shared similar levels of awareness and understanding might find that, at a certain point in the relationship, one partner feels that it no longer aligns with their desires.

In such situations, self-love must be respected and given the time and space it deserves to advocate for your well-being, helping you make the best decision for yourself and the relationship.

Allow me to share a personal example from my first marriage, which serves as a testament to the importance of self-love and self-respect in making life-altering decisions. I married my first boyfriend, and our journey began with a mixture of experiences. We believed we loved each other, and had our share of fun times, but also encountered difficulties, much like any other relationship. It is worth noting that, in the cultural context I was raised in, there were strict rules and limitations. I could not openly have a boyfriend and publicly announce it. I carried the label of a 'good girl' who should not and would not engage in such relationships. The concept of having a boyfriend was virtually unthinkable for those around me, largely due to this label.

Nonetheless, as a young and rebellious individual, I yearned to explore my own path, regardless of external expectations. So, I discreetly ventured into a relationship, keeping it a secret from my parents. They eventually caught wind of my boyfriend in the worst possible manner—through the morality police. One day, we were merely sitting in the park, talking, and the morality police caught us, and took us to the police station; they called my parents, asking, "Do you know where your daughter is?" This question was the epitome of dread for my father, living in Iran around 2008. He replied that he did not know, and they proceeded to inform him that she was conversing with a boy in the park, equating this to her being a prostitute (if not worse)—a grave accusation. Consequently, my parents resorted to threats, including barring me temporarily from going to university and restricting my freedom. My mother, on this occasion, physically reprimanded me, and I could see the anger in my father's eyes. It was an agonising period, and I refrained from speaking to my boyfriend for eight months.

However, I eventually resumed the relationship after enduring numerous ups and downs, all while grappling with the reality that having a boyfriend was not enough—I was compelled to marry him. Despite my internal resistance and knowing it was the wrong path, we went ahead with the wedding, the invitations having already been sent. My parents reluctantly agreed to this union, and I found myself in a marriage I knew was a mistake.

For two years, I scoured for ways to extricate myself from this situation. I applied for PhD programs worldwide, seeking scholarships, and this eventually provided my escape route. I divorced my husband after securing a scholarship in Australia. Looking back now, it is as if Steve Jobs' notion of connecting the dots resonates with me, but through the lens of self-love and self-respect.

I do not wish to paint my ex-husband in a negative light. Instead, what I want to emphasise is that our paths diverged at a certain point. I felt this personally, and perhaps he did too but was in a state of denial. However, at a critical juncture, he let go, and we separated. He did not talk to me during the divorce process. After obtaining my scholarship and firmly expressing my desire to move forward, I obtained a divorce and my visa to Australia within a week. I was about to lose that scholarship and I applied for a two-week extension which was a maximum that my university would grant.

I acknowledge the price I paid, as I arrived in Australia with minimal funds, having sold my possessions to cover the cost of plane tickets and international student insurance. Nevertheless, I wore a wide grin because I knew I had made the right decision, regardless of the price. This experience reinforced the importance of self-love and self-respect in steering the course of one's life and making choices that align with personal growth and happiness.

Self-love and self-respect were the beacons that guided me out of a relationship that was no longer serving my best interests. It is important to recognise that it was not solely self-love and self-respect at play; there were numerous complex, interwoven factors that contributed to this decision. However, at the heart of it all, I believe it was my unwavering self-respect and my willingness to listen to the voice within me that whispered, "This is not working. It is time to move on."

This journey was filled with countless conversations, ups and downs, and numerous challenges, particularly considering the societal norms and obstacles women face in Iran when seeking a divorce. It was a path that demanded great resolve, pitting me against my parents, my ex-husband, and society at large. It required me to navigate a labyrinth of difficulties, including the struggle to assert my desire for a divorce. All of this came at a price, a price I paid in the form of emotional turmoil, persistence, and unwavering determination.

With resolute self-love, self-respect, and a fierce commitment to my own well-being, I embarked on a relentless pursuit of my dreams. This entailed applying to over a hundred universities, seeking scholarships, liquidating my assets, and investing all I had in the pursuit of a new life and a brighter future. The journey ultimately led to my realisation and achievement of the goals I had envisioned for myself. I left behind my familiar surroundings and embarked on a journey to a different continent, armed with nothing but two suitcases and an indomitable spirit. Through it all, it was my deep love for myself, the unwavering respect I held for my own aspirations, and the profound honour I bestowed upon my own journey that lit the path to a new chapter in my life.

Once you have identified the reasons propelling your journey of self-transformation, often encapsulated under the umbrella terms of self-love and self-respect, the subsequent steps involve acknowledging that: you possess an oceanic potential within yourself; that you don't know; and that you are not a tree.

Oceanic Potential

Amidst the darkest days of my life, I embarked on a quest for assurance. I longed to hear that I was not alone, that there existed another version of reality, a reality where I was not solitary in my contemplation of a new way of life. During one of my visits to a wise dervish, he fixed his gaze upon me and uttered, "Ellie, your mother is gripped by fear. In her mind's eye, she envisions you as a wingless bird, destined for peril in the wilderness. Yet, what I perceive within you is a magnificent, majestic bird, endowed with robust wings. Regardless of how high the tree branch you perch upon, should you descend, your wings will carry you aloft. Not everyone possesses the sight to behold these hidden wings, not even you. But I assure you."

This brief exchange unfolded amidst my personal turmoil. I found myself in the throes of a tumultuous struggle for freedom, navigating the complexities of a pending divorce while concurrently seeking PhD opportunities and scholarships across the globe. I was caught in a relentless whirlwind, oscillating between hope and despair. During such trying moments, I unfailingly sought solace in the wisdom of my elderly, enlightened confidant, whose presence in my life had manifested through serendipity, mystical forces, and the embodiment of experience.

This unique connection and the profound imagery he bestowed upon me served as a lifeline during my darkest hours. It resonated deeply, offering a counterpoint to the prevailing narrative of helplessness and dependency that society had woven around me. The prevailing image was one of a fragile, wingless bird, incapable of self-sufficiency and perpetually reliant on the support of others. However, there was another reality—one that recognised my boundless potential, my robust wings that had gone unnoticed. These words instilled in me the conviction to acknowledge, appreciate, and rely upon these latent strengths.

As time unfurled its tapestry of days and years, I delved deeper into the profound essence of this imagery. Knowledge is a multifaceted entity, with its depths unveiling themselves as we journey through life, gaining awareness and consciousness. In the act of penning these words, my appreciation for this profound metaphor has only grown. I am now compelled to share this revelation with all of you—a revelation of your own oceanic potential and the powerful wings that may yet remain undiscovered within you.

Life unfolds with many elements beyond our control. Our place of birth, the parents we inherit, and the societal and cultural backdrop that shapes us are but a few examples. As children, our influence over these aspects is limited, and we navigate our early years with little authority to shape our surroundings. However, the transition into adulthood, which often commences during adolescence, signifies a pivotal juncture. The age at which we assume control varies, contingent upon the knowledge and awareness at our disposal. But what remains consistent is the moment we become masters of our fate, choosing where we reside, the professions we pursue, and the company we keep.

This is the juncture I wish to emphasise—a time when we confront our oceanic potential, a potential accessible to every individual on this planet. The moment to recognise, embrace and wield this power. We bear the responsibility not only to acknowledge the existence of this potential but also to harness it. Take, for instance, the thousands of thoughts that permeate our minds daily. We wield absolute authority over the nature of these thoughts, and the ability to replace and refine them. This is a colossal potential, one facet of our oceanic potential that often goes untapped. We should not surrender to the capricious ebb and flow of thoughts; rather, we must exercise discipline, observe, and filter our thoughts.

Our thoughts exert a profound influence over our habits, moulding our identity, and driving our actions and reactions. On the surface, they may appear as mere fleeting notions, oscillating between reminiscing the past and envisaging the future, engendering mental conversations and conjuring memories. But beneath the surface, they possess a dynamic potency. Our thoughts are the gatekeepers, deciding whether we remain stagnant or journey forward. When harnessed judiciously, they become our staunch allies in crafting the best version of ourselves, propelling us towards the envisioned future self we have long harboured.

The building blocks of our future selves are fashioned from these thoughts, and they represent a fragment of the oceanic potential accessible to all, regardless of their circumstances or past experiences. We must acknowledge this potential and leverage it to its fullest extent, for failing to do so is akin to squandering a boundless treasure.

Imagine the wisdom of my beloved mentor, a brief yet profound encounter during my time in Iran. He compared me to a majestic bird with formidable wings, urging me to recognise my access to the oceanic potential within. It is as if you possess a hidden treasure, its vastness and possibilities extending beyond your grasp. But hear me when I say, that you indeed have those powerful wings, and no matter how high the branches or what adversities may come your way, you can rely on them. You can soar to incredible heights, ascending above the clouds, drawing closer to the radiant sun. You have that potential, though those around you may not always affirm it, and even you might harbour doubts. Yet, I assure you, you hold this boundless oceanic potential within.

To unlock its power, you must believe in yourself and strive to reach the pinnacles that linger in your thoughts, those dreams, wishes, and hopes. Plan, act, harness your strength, and set sail towards your aspirations. Your oceanic potential is a vast reservoir waiting to be tapped. Consider the example of managing your thoughts. Consciously and wisely filter your thoughts, for they shape how you perceive the world and yourself. They create your mental filters, moulding your self-image. Therefore, exercise meticulous thought selection, for these thoughts determine the lens through which you assess the world and shape your destiny. Choose your thoughts deliberately, lest this extraordinary potential remains untapped, a treasure left undiscovered.

I Don't Know

The admission of not knowing something is a crucial step towards embracing wisdom. It requires a substantial dose of courage to utter those three simple words: 'I don't know.' Often, the fear of appearing ignorant or foolish keeps us from acknowledging our lack of knowledge. Yet, it is precisely those individuals who possess self-confidence and self-respect who are more likely to express uncertainty. There is a recognition that this vast universe harbours an abundance of mysteries, knowledge, and awareness, making it perfectly acceptable not to have all the answers.

Contemplating this duality—that we are both a minuscule part of the universe and, simultaneously, the entire universe itself—demands a certain level of awareness, a guiding glimmer of insight. Once you grasp this paradox, the phrase 'I don't know' becomes less of a stumbling block and more a sign of humility and self-acceptance. When you admit, 'I don't know,' you are essentially embracing your own imperfection, and you are entirely at peace with it.

Moreover, saying 'I don't know' is a testament to your readiness to seek assistance, conduct thorough research, delve into various sources, even those that might contradict each other, in your quest to uncover your own truth. You are unafraid to reach out to experts or engage in meaningful conversations with those possessing greater experience and knowledge. It is a trait that exudes a unique kind of humility.

In my view, individuals who have the audacity to utter those three words, 'I don't know,' deserve a special level of respect and admiration. They are the kind of people who recognise that wisdom begins with the acknowledgment of what one doesn't know and who embrace the lifelong journey of learning, self-discovery, and growth.

Exploring the concept of 'I don't know' brings us to another crucial point: the danger of possessing only a smattering of knowledge on a particular topic. This fragmentary knowledge can sometimes be misleading because it often remains on the surface, acquired hastily and without delving deeply. When discussing a subject, it is essential to recognise that one may have only scratched the surface in terms of understanding. It is vital to admit, 'I have begun learning about this, and my knowledge is quite limited. Nevertheless, I am eager to expand my understanding, to learn more, and to delve into the depths of this topic.'

This perspective aligns with the wisdom of the Austrian philosopher Ludwig Wittgenstein, who asserted that 'to understand is to know what to do.' The implication is that true understanding goes hand in hand with knowing how to act. Until one reaches a point where they know precisely what to do, they have not yet attained a profound understanding. It is crucial to recognise that understanding operates on different levels, and the depth of understanding varies according to the topic or concept in question. Therefore, the journey of understanding often begins with acknowledging, 'I don't know,' then progresses to 'I know a little bit,' followed by 'I am reading, pondering, contemplating, and thinking about this,' and finally, 'I am in the process of acquiring knowledge to determine what I want to do with my life, a specific aspect of my life, or a particular habit.' This intricate, multifaceted journey reflects the different levels of comprehension as we navigate the seas of knowledge and understanding.

Moreover, the layers of understanding continue to unfold as we grow and delve deeper into our quest for knowledge. The way we approach things, the actions we take, and the decisions we make undergo transformation along the way. However, it is when we reach the point of crystal-clear clarity and have a distinct purpose that our genuine understanding truly begins to take shape.

As you prepare to articulate what you intend to do based on your understanding, let's turn to the wisdom of one of history's greatest scientists, Albert Einstein. He proposed a framework of five cognitive levels, which are as follows: 5. Smart, 4. Intelligent, 3. Brilliant, 2. Genius, 1. Simple. Surprisingly, the fifth level, 'simple,' is the pinnacle of understanding, while the first level, 'smart,' represents the least depth of comprehension. In essence, the better you grasp a concept, the simpler your solution to it becomes.

This concept of simplicity should not be misconstrued as negating the inherent complexity and intricacies of life, along with the complex solutions life often demands. Rather, it indicates the profound depth of understanding. When you genuinely comprehend a problem, whether it is a troublesome habit or a thought pattern in need of improvement, the solution can be expressed in simple, practical terms. This simplicity lies in the ability to break down a complex solution into manageable, straightforward steps. By doing so, you gain a clear understanding of the next steps required to reach your desired self, your objectives, and your plans.

It is important to note that these cognitive levels suggested by Einstein are not meant for self-analysis or categorisation. The goal is not to ponder whether you are now 'smart,' 'intelligent,' or 'brilliant.' Instead, Einstein's insight serves as a reminder that understanding can be gauged by how simply you can define a problem and propose a straightforward solution. Take some time for introspection and contemplate aspects of your life with which you are dissatisfied. Approach this exercise with honesty, delving into the depths of your understanding. Ask yourself how simply you can state the problem and how simply you can envision a solution for it. This reflection can unveil your true level of understanding.

You Are Not a Tree

Life sometimes blesses us with profound realisations that have the power to alter the trajectory of our existence. One such revelation for me was the deep understanding that I am not to a tree, rooted in my circumstances, unable to break free. Instead, I recognised that I possessed the capacity to move, to embark on a different journey, and to become something entirely new. I understood that I could choose new destinations, and surround myself with different faces, and, most importantly, I held the power and agency to reshape the course of my life. As I have detailed in this book, the society I was born into and the upbringing I received were profoundly restrictive, rooted in fear, and designed to convince me that I was ensnared in an unbreakable web of destiny. My early marriage, a choice made in my youth, was deemed irrevocable. This mentality, deeply ingrained in my culture, defined my worldview.

But then, a pivotal realisation dawned upon me—the understanding that I was not a tree. I comprehended that change was possible, even though it would be a challenging endeavour. This philosophical shift fundamentally transformed my perspective on life. It reshaped the way I perceived myself and altered my self-image. Armed with this newfound insight, I summoned the courage to break free from a loveless marriage and overcome the limiting beliefs that had entrapped me. I resolved to leave behind my homeland, even though the prevailing beliefs suggested there was no escape. This perspective, understanding that I was not rooted like a tree, was a turning point that propelled me forward. It emboldened me to apply for PhD positions worldwide, to stand up for my rights, and ultimately, to embark on the quest to discover my authentic self. It was clear that education was my ticket out, and it was only by disentangling myself from the oppressive grip of my marriage, my homeland, and the continent itself, that I could hope to pursue the light, nourishment, and fertile soil I needed for personal growth. This transformative revelation set the course for my future journey.

In its brevity, this simple sentence carries profound wisdom, evolving into a life philosophy for me. It resonates with the idea that we can alter the circumstances of our lives at any given moment. This philosophy emphasises the innate human ability to change, to adapt, and to grow. We are not like trees, rooted in one place, restricted by the environment in which we are planted. As humans, we possess the extraordinary capacity to think, to transform ourselves, and to redefine our existence.

The power to change is embedded within us, as is the power to alter our thought processes, actions, and self-perception. This realisation opens the door to endless possibilities, allowing us to evolve into individuals unrecognisable to those who knew us just a few years ago. It is a recognition of our oceanic potential, an immense wellspring of capability available to every individual. Once you grasp this understanding, it becomes imperative to harness it to its full extent, to leverage this potential to become who you aspire to be, someone you have always dreamed of becoming. In essence, by embracing the concept that we are not trees, we affirm ourselves as victors in our own life stories. This is not an audacious claim but rather an acknowledgment of the immense wisdom and life lessons encapsulated within this single sentence. It speaks to our inherent agency, our boundless potential, our intrinsic power, and our majesty as human beings.

Now, take a moment to reflect on your own life and identify the areas where the profound wisdom of 'you're not a tree' can be applied. It might be your financial situation, your place of residence, your relationships, your career, your physical and mental well-being, your psychological and spiritual health, or even habits like smoking or gossiping. The message is clear: You are not rooted in place, and you possess the power, techniques, and potential to effect transformation in any aspect of your life at any time.

This message carries profound wisdom and serves as a guiding light for anyone prepared to delve into the depths of self-discovery, prepared to acknowledge the potential for change and transformation. In this simple yet profound sentence, 'you are not a tree,' lies a world of possibilities waiting to be explored. I am eager to learn how you will react and how you will incorporate this life philosophy into your own personal journey of growth and transformation.

After articulating your reasons for self-transformation, acknowledging your oceanic potential, and recognising the limitation of your current knowledge, understanding that you are not fixed like a tree, it is time to cultivate curiosity, harness your imagination, and write your statement of purpose.

Curiosity

Curiosity has always been a driving force in my life; a quality that found its roots back when I was a child. In those days, my brother and I would eagerly explore the streets and alleys near our home on his green bicycle. Summer days were synonymous with endless cycling adventures, where we would trade the handlebars from morning to evening. The sheer joy of it was incomparable, a sensation that stayed with me for a long time.

However, my carefree days of cycling came to a halt as I grew older, particularly when I reached the age of puberty in accordance with Islamic traditions. Suddenly, I found myself bound by certain limitations; the streets were no longer a playground for me. I was expected to follow a set of rules, and guidelines dictating my behaviour, interactions, and dress code.

I questioned these newfound restrictions, both internally and with my parents. Why could I not ride a bicycle like my brother? Why were football games with the neighbourhood boys off-limits? The answers I received were always rooted in tradition, religion, and societal norms. My parents, at that time, with the best intentions, believed that these rules were the way things should be.

Yet, beneath it all, my curiosity and inquisitiveness persisted. I continued to question the norms imposed on me. Over the years, my perspective evolved, and my society changed too. Now, as I engage in conversations with my father, he expresses regret over not allowing me to fully explore my childhood. He wishes he had let me be me, unrestricted by my gender, and permitted me to embrace the carefree joy of being a kid, free to play outside, cycle, and have fun.

Understanding my parents' perspective as well as my own journey, I am grateful for this realisation. I appreciate that my father now acknowledges the importance of allowing a child to be themselves and make their own decisions, simply being a kid.

As a parent now, I find myself embracing a different perspective, one deeply rooted in the desire to foster my daughter's curiosity and self-expression. I consider myself profoundly fortunate to have brought her into this world in a country as free and diverse as Australia. It is a place where she can truly explore her interests, wear what she chooses, and become whoever she aspires to be. While she may not yet comprehend the full extent of this privilege, I, with my distinct life experiences and as her mother, fully grasp it.

I am overjoyed to provide her with the space to be curious, make her own decisions, and simply be herself. In my capacity as a parent, I do my utmost to avoid imposing any religious, ideological, or philosophical restrictions that would hinder her natural exploration. My approach is rooted in allowing her the freedom to explore her potential, to be the architect of her own life, while always ensuring her safety.

My role, as I see it, is that of a supportive companion on her unique journey. I strive to facilitate her pursuit of dreams and passions, fostering her sense of agency and independence. Even though our life experiences differ significantly, I observe her unfettered development with profound appreciation and happiness. While she may not yet fully grasp the depth of her own freedom and possibilities, I am here to encourage and empower her every step of the way.

Curiosity is the unquenchable thirst within us, an insatiable yearning to explore the depths of knowledge, to unearth the mysteries of life. Unlike mere questioning, curiosity bears a distinctly positive connotation, embodying the spirit of inquiry and the pursuit of understanding. It delves into the realm of critical thinking, challenging the status quo and refraining from accepting things at face value.

In the realm of personal transformation and self-improvement, curiosity stands as an indispensable pillar. Consider the boundless inquisitiveness of young children, a constant stream of questions seeking to fathom the world around them. No matter the answers they receive, their appetite for knowledge only grows stronger, propelling them to delve even deeper.

Curiosity is an intrinsic part of our human psyche, woven into the tapestry of our collective consciousness. Unfortunately, as we traverse the path of adulthood, this vibrant sense of curiosity tends to wither. It often wanes in the face of persistent questioning and rigorous critical analysis, overshadowing the childlike wonder that once fuelled our thirst for understanding. Yet, within each of us, this innate curiosity endures, ready to be reignited and harnessed as a powerful force for exploration and growth.

The importance of curiosity becomes evident when we reflect on our childhood. As children, our minds brim with curiosity, and we question the intricacies of the world around us. We ponder the mechanics of our bodies, the development of language, our behavioural responses in various situations, and the way we perceive our emotions. Children are naturally inquisitive, seeking answers to the myriad questions that spring forth in their lives. In most cases, it is the adults, older peers, and teachers surrounding them who provide these answers. However, children lack the resources, reading abilities, comprehension, and skills to independently seek answers.

This is when a significant transformation occurs. The responses, explanations, and ideologies presented to children become imprinted in their developing minds. They become socialised into distinct ways of thinking, understanding, reacting, and living, forming the foundation of their belief systems and ideologies. As adults, we have access to abundant resources, encompassing critical thinking, diverse perspectives, lived experiences, theories, and ideologies. We possess the means to find answers and navigate the vast sea of knowledge at our disposal. The most profound distinction between children and curious adults lies in the adults' access to these resources.

However, rekindling one's curiosity as an adult can be a challenging endeavour. Adults have already been deeply entrenched in a socialisation process that has imprinted numerous beliefs and ideas upon them. Therefore, a curious adult must revisit these imprints, meticulously examining and questioning each one. This deep analysis involves contemplation, wonder, and self-reflection. The adult must decide whether these deeply ingrained concepts, beliefs, and feelings about themselves and the world still serve a purpose. They must determine if these notions align with their desired direction of personal change.

Depending on the individual's upbringing and the ideologies they were exposed to during childhood, this process can range from moderately difficult to exceedingly challenging. The quality of the answers they were provided with as children significantly impacts the extent of the transformation that lies ahead.

In some fortunate cases, individuals are privileged and grow up in families that instil them with positive, supportive, and loving values, beliefs, and ideologies. These individuals have the luxury of choice, allowing them to decide for themselves how to act, react, and shape their lives. However, it is important to acknowledge that this is not the reality for the majority of people. For the rest of us, there is work to be done, a journey to embark on. The first step is curiosity—a profound curiosity that delves into every facet of our being.

We must explore all the beliefs, values, ideologies, and ideas that have been imprinted upon us, questioning how we should be, act, react, feel, and love. This probing is not an act of criticism; it is a genuine exploration. We wonder about the origins of these imprints and whether they truly serve us on our personal journey. It is undoubtedly time-consuming, requiring energy and persistence, but it is a transformative process.

While on this journey, you may encounter pain as you realise how you have been influenced or impacted by your upbringing, your society, and your education system. Yet, it is crucial to remember that this process is not about blame. If feelings of resentment arise, acknowledge them, forgive the source, and refocus on your purpose. Keep your statement of purpose in mind and concentrate on what is within your control. Focus on your ideal future self and work towards that vision.

Indulging in blame is a sidetrack, a diversion from your precious time and energy, and it will not serve your greater goals. Throughout this journey of curiosity and self-discovery, remember that your purpose is personal growth, not resentment or shifting responsibility to others. Your energy is best spent on personal transformation, not dwelling on past influences. Stay committed to the path of self-exploration for it leads to a better, more authentic you.

Imagination

Every night, before slipping into slumber, I embarked on a remarkable journey within the corridors of my imagination. My eyes would often glisten with unshed tears, my mind open to a vast realm of possibilities. In my mind's eye, a recurring image took shape: I envisioned myself seated by an aeroplane window, gazing out into the boundless sky, painted with wisps of white clouds and the hues of a hopeful sunrise. In this mental reverie, I wore the fatigue of life's struggles and the weight of unfulfilled dreams, yet a glimmer of glory and boundless hope danced in my heart. This vision was my refuge, my self-constructed sanctuary from the disheartening reality of my daily existence.

As the sun rose in my imaginative world, my real-life circumstances mirrored a stark contrast. Each day, I diligently applied for opportunities across the globe. My hands tirelessly filled out applications; my voice echoed through phone calls and emails, and my dreams soared on the wings of scholarship opportunities that beckoned from different corners of the world—America, Australia, Canada, England, anywhere that held the promise of a new beginning. Simultaneously, my feet remained grounded in the trials of my existence, navigating the labyrinthine maze of an unfulfilling marriage that had long soured in my heart. The gap between the life I lived and the reality I dreamed of grew with each passing day, but I persevered relentlessly, crafting a plan to bridge that chasm. The visualisations of the aeroplane window served as a beacon of hope during those dark days. They were the architects of an alternate reality that held me aloft amidst life's tempests. Day by day, through unwavering persistence and effort, I inched closer to manifesting my dreams. And when the opportunity finally arrived, in the form of a PhD scholarship, it was nothing short of a lifeline that pulled me from the abyss of despair, granting me a ticket to rebirth in a distant land—Australia, a place whose true essence was a mystery to me.

When I speak of potential as an ever-present gift within each individual's grasp, our boundless realm of imagination emerges as one of its most enchanting facets. Regardless of the constraints imposed by our immediate surroundings, whether within the confines of our homes or the boundaries of our reality, we possess an expansive world of imagination with limitless horizons. It is a realm unfettered by any restrictions, where our minds can conjure and visualise anything, whether within the bounds of our current knowledge or beyond. This powerful tool, this untamed wellspring of potential, yearns to be harnessed and should never be tethered to the limits of our current circumstances.

Have you ever paused to marvel at the notion that we each possess not one, but an infinite canvas within our imagination? A canvas that eagerly awaits the strokes of creativity to paint various versions, distinct lives, and alternate realities for ourselves. The beauty lies in our ability to take those vibrant strokes and transform them into a purposeful plan that bridges the chasm between our present reality and the vivid imagination we have sculpted. Isn't it astonishing to comprehend that this potential exists within us, waiting to be utilised? It is not just awareness; it is a treasure waiting to be uncovered. A treasure, an aspiration that seekers in life are perpetually pursuing. This boundless potential, this oceanic expanse, is a brilliant resource available to anyone, at any given moment. The real magic lies in recognising this reservoir of potential and, more importantly, in embracing the responsibility to employ it for our own betterment.

As I write these lines, I did sit at the window seat of an aeroplane; I did leave Iran. I did win a PhD scholarship in one of the most prestigious universities in the world. I did do my PhD and the person who is writing these lines is completely different from the person, who had that aeroplane visualisation, but the technique is the same; the way is the same. The potential of the imagination is the same. As I write these lines, I have a different desired self in mind. I have a different imagination and I have a different plan and different small steps to realise it, and I am sure that I am going to realise my dreams because once you do it you see that it is possible. Once it happens to you; once you see that it is working you believe it and then you use it as a tool; you use it as a resource; you use it as a treasure; you utilise it in the best way you can, because if you do not use it, it is going to go to waste; and you are going to be trapped in your automated, autopilot life, and you are going to stay where you are if you are lucky; if not, you are going to move backwards; your life is going to deteriorate.

Statement of Purpose

Amidst the quiet solitude of my study, I find myself leafing through the dusty pages of my old notebooks, each one a treasure trove of my past aspirations. As my eyes drift across the written declarations, I am transported back to various junctures in my life, each marked by a distinct statement of purpose. These are the whispered promises I made to myself as I embarked on a relentless journey of self-transformation, spanning several chapters of my existence.

One of these statements boldly proclaims, 'I am a multibillionaire.' Another, inked beside it, reads, 'I have secured a visa for my parents to visit Australia.' It is the latter that stirs a tempest of memories within me. A turbulent era, approximately a decade ago, where I found myself ensnared in the confines of a loveless marriage, with the shadows of despair closing in. It was a time when escape seemed nigh impossible, but hope existed within the sanctuary of my own imagination. A glimmer of salvation was concealed within the confines of my knowledge.

This knowledge, a beacon in my darkest hours, attested to my ability to break free from the chains that bound me. My academic journey had already culminated in the attainment of a master's degree, and I knew that international PhD opportunities awaited, scattered across the globe. These were not mere slots in distant universities; they were gateways to the world, each accompanied by a scholarship that would pave my way.

One could argue that my statement of purpose was not meticulously articulated in the form of 'I will leave Iran via a PhD scholarship.' However, the declaration lived within my nightly visualisations, etched vividly in my mind's eye. Each night, as I lay down to rest, I would conjure images of myself on an aeroplane, my head uncovered, and a radiant smile adorning my face. In those reveries, I was leaving behind a land, a marriage, and a past shrouded in darkness, and I was hurtling towards a luminous future.

During these visualisations, I would be suffused with a palpable enthusiasm, the buoyant emotions of success, the triumphant conviction that I had indeed persevered. The sun's rays streamed through the aeroplane window, enveloping me in their warmth, and it was not an aircraft that I sat in; I had sprouted wings, morphing into a bird in flight. Light as a feather, I soared on my own powerful wings, the embodiment of freedom. I could sense that all the statements of purpose I had ever penned were inscribed into the very core of my being, seared into the essence of my DNA, imprinted on each cell, and breathed in with every vital, life-sustaining breath.

And now, as I transcribe these words, I feel the resonance of those emotions reverberating within me. I understand the profound influence that a statement of purpose can wield, not only when inked on paper but also when etched into the very fibres of our physical and metaphysical selves. This is what I desired; this is what I would attain. The significance of these nightly visualisations, fuelled by discipline and persistence, is something I am only now beginning to comprehend.

At this moment, as I lay bare my introspections upon this page, I am awash with a sense of pride. Pride in my dedication to those visualisations; pride in the unwavering faith that what I had visualised, I had indeed realised. I am overwhelmed by the sense of responsibility to translate this wisdom into words and share it with every reader who holds this book in their hands.

Embarking on a journey of self-improvement and transformation requires a clear and unwavering statement of purpose. This statement, concise and focused, serves as your guiding star, not just during the high-energy, triumphant days but also in the depths of despair, when motivation wanes, and the shadows loom large. Those challenging moments are an integral part of the transformation path, and the statement of purpose becomes your constant companion, inscribed in your consciousness. As you evolve and grow, your statement of purpose evolves with you, an ever-shifting beacon illuminating your way.

Incorporating the practice of journaling in your transformation journey is of paramount importance. By chronicling your thoughts, habits, beliefs, and the evolving aspects of your life, you create a tangible record of your progress. Picture this: A year has passed, and you find yourself reflecting on your initial statement of purpose, your starting point. You review the myriad changes you have embraced, drawing nearer to your goals and the person you aspire to become. With clarity, you discern the next steps needed to inch closer to your desired destination.

However, it is crucial to recognise that there is no ultimate destination. Life's journey is a paradoxical blend of setting goals, working towards them, and understanding that each destination reached merely marks the beginning of a new one. This concept may require time and depth to fully grasp, but from my personal experience, I can attest to its truth: we are perpetual travellers on an ever-unfolding journey of transformation. It is not about reaching a final destination but about embracing the process, for as the famous saying goes, *Each pinnacle is both the end and the start of another mountain.*

Set your sights on a timeframe for your statement of purpose; be it a six-month commitment, a year-long endeavour, or even a lifetime mission. You hold the reins of your choices, allowing you to craft statements of purpose for short, medium, and long terms. This process, however, can be simplified by beginning with a single statement of purpose. The key lies in anchoring it with a clear timeframe, as I have emphasised before. Understand that this statement is not set in stone; rather, it is a dynamic reflection of your ever-evolving self.

Transcribe your statement of purpose into your journal or inscribe it with your own hand, tangible proof of your dedication. Print it out, place it where you cannot ignore it, and let it be your daily reminder of why you set foot on this transformative journey. In times of hardship, when the path ahead seems bleak and the fruits of your labour remain elusive, your statement of purpose becomes your sanctuary. Recite it aloud, meditate on it, and rekindle the embers of your motivation. Pause and reflect on the growth you have achieved and the positive changes you have witnessed. Remind yourself of the profound reasons that initiated this journey.

Remember, it is entirely acceptable to grant yourself a day of rest when needed. We all require moments of respite. Yet, the key lies in your return, the resumption of your journey. After a brief interlude, ensure you rise once more. Put your hand to your heart, and on the morrow, get back on the path of self-transformation. I advocate for these brief respites, acknowledging that sometimes the journey can become overwhelming or fear may cast a shadow. A single day of rest is permissible, but I discourage extended hiatuses, for the principles of consistency and discipline are the bedrock of transformation.

Each day is a link in the chain of your transformation journey, and it is imperative to add one more circle to that chain every day.

This statement of purpose weds the formidable strength of initiating a self-transformation journey with the enduring power of the written word. It underlines the profound significance of journaling and the enlightening act of reflecting on the path we have thus far traversed. As we delve into the narratives of our transformative journey, we focus on what has transpired thus far, on the catalyst that ignited this path of self-transformation. Through these written records, we gain an infusion of extraordinary energy and resilience. This is not merely a reminiscence of our journey; it is a powerful reminder of our potential, a reaffirmation of our belief in our dreams, and a rekindling of our resolve to evolve.

Within every reader of these lines resides a wellspring of immense potential, waiting to be unlocked. The degree to which you unleash this potential is contingent on your readiness, the depth of your knowledge, and your awareness. Armed with this knowledge, you can embark on your own unique journey, an odyssey as individual as you are. Drawing from your life experiences, the wisdom you have accrued, and the knowledge you possess, you carve a path distinct from any other. Your journey depends on the fire of your persistence, the anchor of your discipline, and the depth to which you tap into your latent potential.

Embrace the notion that every individual's journey is inherently unique, just as your statement of purpose is exclusively yours. Allow it to evolve and transform with you, reflecting your growth and aspirations. Be mindful that the journey is an on-going saga, punctuated by moments of rest and reflection. If a one-day hiatus is what you need, grant yourself that pause, but always find your way back to the compelling narrative of your transformation. Resume your visionary journey, your meticulous planning, your journaling, your writing, and above all, your continued ascent to shine and thrive. And above all, start with a statement of purpose.

After you write down your statement of purpose, tapping into your curiosity and imagination, this is the moment when fears surface, and uncertainty looms large. The next step is to embrace this uncertainty and cultivate mental toughness.

Fear: The Hesitant Shadow

Within the four letters of 'fear,' an intricate and formidable obstacle to human potential resides. It's the trepidation that often halts us in our tracks, casting doubt upon our abilities and dreams.

In our earliest days, fear is an unfamiliar concept. We are born with unbridled courage, fearless in our exploration of the world. But as we grow, as life introduces us to both genuine threats and imagined dangers, fear takes root in our hearts.

Parents, driven by love and the instinct to protect, can unwittingly become the architects of this fear. Their well-intentioned vigilance can inadvertently sow the seeds of hyper-vigilance and apprehension within their children.

Throughout my own life's journey, I have frequently been labelled as 'shy' and 'cautious.' These descriptors, like ink on paper, have been used to sketch my character, yet I question whether they were imprinted upon me from birth or painted by my parents' well-intended aspirations of raising a 'good girl.' It's a riddle that still eludes a definitive answer.

As I stand on the precipice of my 36th year, I can't help but notice that the veil of reserve still drapes over me. However, it's a shapeshifting quality, adapting to the context and the emotions that define a moment. Perhaps, in my formative years, I feared shattering the image my parents had crafted, regardless of its authenticity. Or maybe, over the years, I have internalised this persona.

Yet, the spectre of fear persists. It accompanies me when I contemplate taking that first exhilarating plunge into a pool, when I summon the courage to attempt acrobatic feats in aerial yoga, or when I muster the resolve to pursue challenging yoga poses. These paralysing doubts, magnified through the lenses of my glasses, prompt me to ponder how different I might have been without this unwarranted fear as a constant companion.

Today, I see myself as a more intrepid individual, one who actively confronts her fears and strives for personal growth. The journey has commenced, but I'm aware that the path ahead is long and winding.

As a parent, my mantra is straightforward: 'You can do this.' My deepest wish is to endow my daughter with a world where fear holds fewer dominions, a world where she can boldly embrace life's challenges with open arms. However, I'm also cognizant, as every parent is, that the art of parenting is punctuated by its own unique missteps and stumbles along the way.

Embracing an Ever-present Uncertainty

On 10 September 2023, I marked the ninth year of my life in Australia—a decade shaped by migration. I use the term 'home' to describe this land, but my feelings about it are as diverse as the hues of a painter's palette. I find myself dwelling in an enigmatic realm, suspended between two worlds. I am neither purely Iranian nor wholly Australian; my identity straddles these two realms.

Official documents may label me as a citizen of this sunburnt land, but the labyrinth of emotions and questions that swirl within me remains untouched by ink and paper. A decade in Sydney, yet I grapple with the haunting uncertainties of belonging and identity. What if, in the capricious dance of life, I can no longer call Australia home? What if the shadow of return to Iran looms, a prospect I'm reluctant to embrace? These questions, like phantoms, visit me in moments of vulnerability—when I chase a new job as my contract nears its end, or when the weight of our substantial mortgage bears down upon me.

In the midst of such doubts, I remind myself of the journey I have traversed. I have navigated the turbulent currents of life for 36 years, even entering this world as an unwanted child. It's a journey that has forged me, a testament to my resilience and tenacity. The uncertainty that shrouds my life is a constant companion, an ever-present element that shadows us all.

Migrants, like myself, carry the added weight of complex histories, traumas, and the absence of family in this new abode we've chosen to call home. Our lives are spun from the threads of uncertainty, woven into intricate tapestries of existence. Yet, with each trial we overcome, and each challenge we embrace, our resilience grows stronger, illuminating our path with purpose.

COVID-19 has cast an even broader net of uncertainty over the world, weaving the unpredictable into the fabric of daily existence. As migrants, we stand as participants in this global drama, navigating its twists and turns with fortitude.

In the end, I find solace in the knowledge that no matter what uncertainties lie ahead, I am fortified by the strength I have gathered on this odyssey. It is this very resilience that gives meaning to my life—a reminder that we are bound not by the certainties we possess, but by the uncertainties we dare to face. Each uncertainty, though daunting, is a testament to the vibrancy of life itself—a life where I continue to explore the uncharted territory of my identity, seeking answers, embracing growth, and weaving my own narrative amidst the ever-evolving tapestry of existence.

Mental Toughness

In the heart of my transformative fitness journey, the workout room pulsated with energy. The clinks of dumbbells and the rhythmic beat of my trainer's instructions filled the air. My muscles, already pushed to the brink, felt like molten lava, burning with the intensity of the session. Beads of sweat danced down my temples, a testament to the physical exertion coursing through my veins.

Amidst the weights and the echoes of my own heavy breaths, the air was charged with anticipation. "And now," my trainer announced, a spark in her eyes, "two minutes of plank."

I groaned inwardly. Planks were the nemesis, the Everest of core exercises. The room blurred as I dropped to the mat, feeling the cool embrace of its surface against my hot, flushed skin. My trainer's voice became a distant hum, drowned by the internal chatter. "You're tired, let it go," my mind urged, but I knew this was more than a physical challenge. It was a battle of willpower.

"3…2…1…" The countdown initiated a mental switch. The world faded, leaving only the timer ticking down in the periphery. The seconds felt like eternities as I navigated the tumultuous sea of my thoughts. "You can do this. You are stronger than you think. You have got this," I whispered, the words a lifeline.

The room ceased to exist; it was just me and the struggle. Sweat poured like a waterfall, a tangible testament to my commitment. 'I am strong. I am invincible.' The mantra echoed in my ears, drowning out the doubts.

At 1 minute and 10 seconds, my body trembled, the strain threatening to break my resolve. "Shift to one arm," my trainer's voice penetrated the mental fog. The shift brought a fresh wave of intensity.

"I can do this. I've got this," I affirmed, teeth gritted, muscles screaming.

The countdown resumed. "3…2…1…" I collapsed, the coolness of the mat a welcome relief. Exhaustion and triumph intertwined, creating a symphony of sensations. "I did it," I breathed, feeling the pulse of victory course through me.

The room, once a battleground, now bore witness to a personal conquest. The echoes of my heavy breaths lingered, a testament to the hard things endured for the promise of a stronger, more resilient self on the horizon.

Year after year, I meticulously inscribe my goals in the pages of my diary, transforming mere wishes into tangible goals. The evolution of this practice has mirrored my deepening commitment to self-improvement and the pursuit of greatness. Beyond the act of writing, I take the extra step of materialising my ambitions by printing them out and strategically placing them on mirrors and walls throughout my home workspace. I choose this quiet declaration over vocal proclamations, allowing my achievements to resonate louder than any spoken word once they come to fruition. This deliberate approach not only serves as a constant visual reminder but also signifies my unwavering dedication to the on-going journey of goal attainment.

However, understanding the natural human inclination towards ease and comfort, I recognise the need for mental preparation and toughness to break free from the allure of the familiar. Our biological predisposition favours the path of least resistance, a tendency deeply ingrained in our survival instincts. Yet, when committed to the relentless pursuit of self-improvement and achieving greatness, embracing discomfort becomes a prerequisite. Mental preparation, akin to physical conditioning, demands consistent practice to enhance one's mental toughness. It involves a daily ritual of affirmations, reinforcing the belief that I am capable, resilient, and possess an untapped well of potential. Just as one builds physical strength in the gym, the mind requires regular workouts to fortify its resilience. This on-going cultivation of mental toughness becomes the anchor in navigating the challenges that accompany the pursuit of ambitious goals, transforming aspirations into concrete realities.

Once the ink dries on your carefully outlined goals, etched onto the canvas of your aspirations for the upcoming year and beyond, the true odyssey begins. It is not merely about the act of putting pen to paper but delving into the intricate landscape of your mind, preparing it for the challenges ahead. Short-term and long-term goals alike demand mental fortitude and resilience, and this journey necessitates a recalibration of your mindset.

As the goals materialise on paper, a battleground emerges within the recesses of your mind. Limiting beliefs, wavering self-confidence, entrenched fears, and the echoes of societal conditioning surface to cast doubt on your capabilities. In these moments, where the familiar pangs of self-doubt linger, it becomes paramount to assert your potential. To envision a future distinct from your current reality, you must confront these internal adversaries. Mental preparation, coupled with unwavering toughness, becomes your armour against the onslaught of doubt.

Choosing the path less travelled, contrary to our biological predisposition for ease, requires intentional effort. This is the crucible where the strength of your mental preparation shines. It demands an energy exertion not inherent in our natural wiring. Yet, as you consistently reinforce the belief in your capabilities, practice mental toughness, and commit to daily actions aligned with your goals, the once arduous choice of the harder path becomes a conscious, empowering decision. With each intentional step, you are rewiring your neural pathways, making resilience and deliberate choices a second nature. As the days unfold, the journey becomes not just about achieving goals but a testament to the transformative power of a prepared and resilient mind.

Embarking on the path of transformation, especially in the initial stages, unfailingly introduces you to the concept of resistance. Picture waking up earlier, adhering to a daily exercise routine, committing to consistent writing, or adopting a healthier dietary regimen—these endeavours, aligned with your grand vision, are bound to encounter resistance. The resistance, akin to a formidable adversary, attempts to thwart your every move.

In the nascent stages, the tasks may seem Herculean, demanding an extra ounce of effort to overcome the resistance. However, this juncture is where the alchemy of perseverance, discipline, and mental preparation transpires. The key lies in understanding that resistance is not a deterrent but a rite of passage, a necessary phase in your evolution. By persisting through this initial struggle and consciously opting for the more challenging route, your mental toughness is not only honed but fortified.

As the days unfold and your commitment deepens, the once-daunting resistance begins to wane. What seemed insurmountable gradually becomes more manageable, and the energy required to navigate these challenges lessens. The mental preparedness cultivated during this process becomes your compass, guiding you through subsequent endeavours. Acknowledge the inevitability of the initial resistance, yet stay attuned to the promise of a transformative payoff.

In this journey, be your own ally, offering patience and understanding. If the need for a brief respite arises, grant it without judgment. Use these interludes not as moments of defeat but as opportunities to recalibrate your mental preparation, reinforcing your mental toughness. Remember, as you persist and navigate through the resistance, the fruits of your labour will manifest, ushering in a new era of achievement and self-discovery.

If the canvas of your life is waiting to be painted with the vibrant strokes of transformation, the brushes of mental preparedness and toughness are indispensable tools. Crafting a new version of yourself, and attaining those dreams that have lingered in the corridors of your mind, demands a willingness to confront and conquer the challenges that lie ahead. In essence, you must be ready to do hard things.

Mental preparedness acts as your compass, guiding you through the labyrinth of sweat, hardship, and the unforeseen. It is an acknowledgment that growth, the journey, and the process require a steadfast resolve to face the difficulties head-on. Just as a chef anticipates the heat and effort required to create a world-class meal, your mental preparedness is the prerequisite for the extraordinary feast of self-transformation you're about to cook.

Consider this truth: the more you embrace and conquer difficult challenges, the easier it becomes to set loftier goals and tackle even more formidable tasks. This isn't merely about enduring hardship; it is about evolving into a person capable of navigating the intricate dance between ambition and accomplishment. Remember, greatness is not forged in the crucible of simplicity. Therefore, embrace the idea of working hard, but also, crucially, working smart.

Let it be known that the call to 'toughen up' is not a simplistic mantra; it is an invitation to fortify your mental resilience, to build a foundation that can withstand the storms of life. As you embark on this transformative journey, consider mental toughness not as a burdensome weight but as the armour that will empower you to scale the peaks of your aspirations. The work ahead is challenging, yet the rewards are boundless—so, toughen up, for there is a masterpiece waiting to be sculpted, and you are its architect.

After embracing uncertainty and cultivating mental toughness, it's time to address our habits—the cornerstones of our lives—and reshape how we navigate our daily existence.

Habits

Habits play a fundamental role in our lives, impacting our self-development and life transformation. It is hard to fathom that any book on these topics could overlook the pivotal role that habits play. We engage in countless activities daily out of habit, and these habits often take root in our early years, heavily influenced by our surroundings.

The circumstances of our birth and upbringing significantly shape the habits we acquire. Our family, the environment we are born into, and the behaviours we observe all have a profound impact on our early life habits. This creates a distinct element of privilege or disadvantage in our habits. For instance, being born into a family that regularly consumes fruits and vegetables establishes a positive habit that can benefit an individual throughout their life. Conversely, growing up in a household where late-night heavy dinners are the norm can lead to unhealthy habits that are challenging to overcome.

Habits are, in essence, tools designed to serve a purpose. They facilitate the automation of daily activities, conserving our mental and physical energy. Remarkably, nearly everything we do, from the moment we awaken in the morning to the choices we make for breakfast, the people we engage with, and how we express our emotions, is governed by habits. These habits dictate the way we dress, speak, and even our tone of voice.

Recognising that the majority, if not all, of our lives are governed by habits underscores the immense significance of understanding and cultivating positive, constructive habits. For those who were not fortunate enough to be exposed to such habits early in life, the journey towards personal growth and transformation becomes more challenging. In such cases, we must be ready to learn and unlearn, shedding habits that no longer serve us.

As we become more self-aware and committed to change, we can take control of our lives by consciously reshaping our habits. This journey requires dedication and investment, but it holds the key to a more fulfilling and purpose-driven life.

Developing new habits and breaking free from old ones is a substantial undertaking that demands unwavering energy, focus, persistence, and investment. Establishing a fresh habit is a labour-intensive process, and unlearning an old one to make way for a new habit can be even more time-consuming and energy-draining. It requires a significant amount of work, effort, and discipline. The difficulty of this endeavour is such that not everyone succeeds in acquiring new positive and productive habits, let alone in shedding those that no longer align with their envisioned life path and personal growth journey.

There is often inertia associated with forming or replacing habits, and it is a common and understandable challenge. I can personally relate to the struggle. However, once we recognise that a particular habit is no longer serving us, we bear the responsibility to either establish a new one if it does not exist or replace an old, unproductive habit with something more beneficial.

I have always admired those who have cultivated the habit of reading regularly, practising a musical instrument, or engaging in artistic pursuits such as painting, pottery, or weaving. I envy those who speak of their early years filled with music, books, art, philosophy, inspiring discussions, open-mindedness, early rising, an appreciation for life, a strong sense of family values, and a commitment to self-development, self-love, and self-respect. These individuals, unafraid to challenge societal norms, inspire me. The early formation of such positive habits carries immense significance, as it paves the way for a fulfilling and purpose-driven life.

However, I also believe that it is never too late to embark on this journey. Once we realise the need for a new habit or the replacement of an outdated one to achieve our life goals and fulfil our dreams and visions, it becomes our responsibility. We must persist, take action, and diligently work on forming new habits or breaking free from the old ones. I find myself mostly belonging to this second group, as I have embarked on the challenging path of unlearning habits from my childhood that were unproductive. This journey has encompassed various aspects of life, from nutritional knowledge and portion control to the thoughts I allow into my mind, self-image, reading habits, self-acceptance, and self-love. It has been a journey of forging new habits and replacing the old ones that no longer serve my aspirations and future vision. And the journey continues as I write these lines.

In the realm of life coaching and personal transformation, habits play a pivotal role. Depending on the specific areas of life one aims to enhance, the habits relevant to those areas must be meticulously scrutinised, contemplated, and analysed. Identifying the roots and causes of these habits is crucial in the process of self-transformation and personal development. Habits hold the power to shape and determine our journey towards self-realisation and personal growth, and it is in their transformation that we truly unlock our potential.

I would like to emphasise a point here: in my opinion, no habit, once we become aware of it and gain knowledge about it, should ever be taken for granted. Each and every habit must be subjected to scrutiny and assessment in the light of our goals and aspirations. When we realise that a particular habit aligns with our objectives and serves a useful purpose, it can remain in our lives. If not, it needs to be replaced, improved, or enhanced in some way. Every habit should go through this filtering process.

Reaching this stage of self-awareness and readiness to evaluate our habits is a continuous and evolving process. It does not happen overnight; it demands time, effort, and energy. It necessitates learning, training, meaningful conversations, reflection, writing, and daily practice. Perseverance and discipline are essential components of this journey. The reward, however, is significant; it is an indispensable part of living a conscious and fulfilling life that we can be proud of.

Now, I would like to delve into the habits that I believe can benefit anyone on their journey of self-development and life transformation.

One of these habits is continuous learning. While learning is a significant part of our formal education, what I am referring to here is personal learning—a deliberate, purpose-driven, and deep exploration of various aspects of life. This encompasses nutrition, physical activity, thought processes, and our overall perspective on life. Continuous learning is a lifelong endeavour, a journey without an end, and it never ceases in my view. This habit involves seeking knowledge from trusted sources, drawing insights from personal experiences, and learning from those who have already walked the path we aspire to follow. Such intentional and continuous learning is invaluable and immensely beneficial at any stage of life. It empowers us to evolve, adapt, and thrive in an ever-changing world, making it a habit that can truly serve individuals on their path to self-improvement and life transformation.

The habit of reading books, closely tied to continuous learning, is undeniably transformative and revolutionary. I often impart to my daughter that there is one thing I would never decline, and that is purchasing new books. I have remained true to this principle, always getting her the books she desires. I firmly believe that investing in books is a type of investment that is never wasted; it pays off in knowledge and personal growth. In fact, I advocate having more books than we can read at a given moment. If a book does not resonate with us, it is perfectly fine to set it aside. If we find a book we love, it is worth reading multiple times, as each reading reveals new depths, meanings, and layers of nuance. Having a book with you wherever you go, delving into its pages, and losing yourself in its world, whether it is a novel or a non-fiction work on topics like finance or self-improvement, is a habit that can enrich our lives.

In today's digital age, listening to books has also become common, offering a convenient alternative to traditional reading. So, whether you are reading or listening to books, having books as companions is an incredible habit that anyone can cultivate.

Another valuable companion in life is fitness, and by fitness, I do not mean just physical fitness; it extends to mental, psychological, and spiritual fitness. Each individual should invest in all these facets throughout their lives, particularly when striving for personal development and self-improvement.

When it comes to physical fitness, it is essential to be mindful of what foods we consume, and their nutritional value. We should keep our bodies in motion because they are designed for activity, not sedentary living. In addition, mental fitness demands time away from electronic devices, granting ourselves moments of silence, meditative reflection, and the precious 'me-time' that allows for mental rejuvenation. Investing in psychological well-being is vital, ensuring our emotional and mental health is in top form.

These various forms of fitness are paramount in one's life. Our bodies and minds are our companions throughout our time on Earth, and it is our responsibility to care for them. In nurturing these habits, we set the stage for becoming a better version of ourselves in every aspect of life, ensuring that we leave a positive and lasting impact on this world.

Another significant habit closely tied to mental fitness is the kind of thoughts we engage with daily, the thoughts we permit into our minds, and how we react to these thoughts. It is of utmost importance to be conscious of our thoughts, to understand their power, and to learn how to think in a more productive and useful manner, aligning with the future we envision for ourselves. Each 24-hour window is a building block towards the goals we set, and during each of these hours, our minds are bustling with numerous thoughts. The nature of these thoughts does not just influence our current circumstances but profoundly shapes the lives we create for ourselves in the future. Therefore, it is paramount to take charge of the thoughts we allow in our minds.

In my personal view, this is so crucial that the art of harnessing our mental power and controlling the thoughts we allow should be a part of our educational curriculum, instilled from early schooling and adapted as our children progress through the education system. Our thoughts can change our mood, reshape our perspective on life, and influence the kind of future we build by the thoughts we entertain or dismiss. Our mental fitness, in essence, is a vital habit that needs to be cultivated, and its significance cannot be overstated in the life of any individual.

Another essential habit is choosing the company we keep wisely. By this, I do not mean seeking those who offer material goods or financial assistance; I am referring to individuals who have something valuable to offer, such as ideas, life experiences, inspiring stories, or even the gift of silence. I have observed how spending time with individuals who can sit in silence for an hour can fill you with energy, inspiration, and positivity. Cultivating the habit of carefully selecting our companions can have an exponential impact on our lives. If there is something like a compound effect in personal growth, it is in having the company of people who provide wisdom, curiosity, new ideas, inspiration, and genuine companionship. Such individuals are like gold in our lives.

But there is an even higher level to this concept: we should strive to become that kind of company ourselves. We should be the companions who share new ideas, inspire others, and offer positivity, along with the fresh insights we have gained from our own experiences. This is the pinnacle of self-awareness, a profound transformation, and a unique level of energy and resonance that an individual can offer as a companion.

Recognising the impact of habits on our lives is crucial during the self-transformation journey. It prompts us to become acutely aware of our existing habits, assess whether they contribute to our productivity and well-being, and decide whether to retain, modify, or discard them in the pursuit of personal evolution.

Breaking Free from Fossilised Beliefs

Unearthing and dismantling long-held, fossilised beliefs can be an exhausting endeavour. These beliefs, some of which never truly served me, were thrust upon me during my vulnerable, formative years.

Let's delve into an example that strikes a universal chord—religion. I was born into a family that adhered to Islamic principles, which meant I was steeped in the customs of covering my hair, offering prayers, fasting, preserving my chastity, and the ominous threats of divine consequences for disobedience. As a child, I found these notions nonsensical, and at times, horrifying. The idea of being condemned to hell for minor transgressions or facing gruesome punishments like being hung by my own hair for exposing it haunted my young mind.

As I embarked on my intellectual journey, akin to Descartes' quest for truth, around the age of eighteen, I began to explore the origins of religion, the concept of choice, and the revelation that I was not beholden to my parents' or society's dictates. It was liberating to realise I had agency, that I could shape my beliefs, and that I didn't have to conform to inherited dogma.

This metamorphosis has been a gradual process, akin to shedding old skin to make way for the new. The awareness I have cultivated over the years, through reading, conversations, and introspection, has been akin to a guiding light piercing through the darkness of unquestioned beliefs. I feel more illuminated by the knowledge I have uncovered, knowing that I have played an active role in this transformation.

It's essential to acknowledge that this transformation is neither swift nor effortless. Challenging deeply ingrained beliefs is taxing and, at times, emotionally draining. However, I remind myself that valuable change often comes at a cost. I'm committed to the arduous journey of re-evaluating my beliefs, redefining my worldview, and understanding my true potential.

This journey has also significantly impacted my approach to parenting. In the realm of religion, my husband and I have chosen not to impose any singular truth on our daughter. We want her to grow up with the freedom to decide her own spiritual path. We've refrained from making choices for her, such as piercing her ears or obtaining Iranian documentation. We want her to exercise her own agency and make these decisions when she's mature enough to do so. This choice may complicate our lives, as it prevents us from travelling to Iran with her, but we believe in empowering her with the gift of choice.

I must confess that parenting, like life itself, is an imperfect journey. We recognise that, at times, our choices may inadvertently harm our children, but we're committed to providing our daughter with a secular upbringing that emphasises choice, agency, and an open-minded perspective from day one. We believe that, to the best of our abilities, we're nurturing her growth into an individual who can navigate the world with confidence, independence, and a thirst for knowledge.

Spring Cleaning

Spring cleaning is a universal concept, transcending cultural boundaries, as it symbolises the season of renewal. Traditionally, people tidy up their physical spaces, dusting and mopping their homes as the new season blossoms. But beyond the tangible act of cleaning, spring cleaning holds a deeper metaphorical significance. It extends to cleansing one's mind and soul of old grievances, grudges, and any lingering negativity. Spring becomes an opportune moment to shed the weight of the past and make room for new growth.

For as long as I can remember, my journey of self-transformation and personal evolution has been a perpetual spring cleaning of the mind. This goes beyond just a seasonal ritual; it is a way of life. I have been continually assessing and revamping my mental landscape, re-evaluating the perspectives and beliefs through which I interpret the world. I have been scrutinising my socialisation, habits, and beliefs, discarding those that no longer align with the path I have chosen. My life resembles an on-going renovation project, with each season marked by new beginnings, fresh insights, and personal growth. This journey of renewal is never-ending, and I am committed to the continuous process of spring cleaning, ensuring that my inner world remains as vibrant as the season itself.

Reflecting on Fossilised Beliefs

In the unfolding chapters of my post-marital journey, liberated from a union that no longer served me, I found myself in the vibrant landscape of Australia, supported by a PhD scholarship. As I navigated this newfound freedom, encountering the diverse individuals, I felt the stirrings of desire, prompting me to explore the realms of dating. The journey held promises of connection, with walks, shared moments of tenderness, and the dance of intimacy awakening within me. However, beneath the surface, a cascade of societal expectations and internalised judgments threatened to cloud these moments.

In the tender embrace of physical arousal, questions echoed in the corridors of my mind, questioning my identity, my goodness, and the potential judgment of those around me. The conflict between personal desires and societal conditioning cast a shadow over the joyous exploration of physical intimacy. Each intimate moment became a battlefield of conflicting thoughts, drowning the experience in a sea of self-doubt. It was a poignant struggle between the desire to heed societal norms and the call of my authentic self.

Feeling the weight of these beliefs, I made a conscious decision to embark on a journey of introspection. Armed with a pen and the resolve to unravel the layers of conditioning, I delved into the roots of these beliefs. Tracing the origins back to the religious teachings that painted the image of a 'good girl' confined within the boundaries of marriage, and the societal echoes reinforcing these limitations, I recognised the stains of judgment that threatened to mar the canvas of my experiences.

As the ink flowed onto the pages of my reflections, I confronted the inherited beliefs that sought to dictate my actions. The narrative, woven by societal norms, began to unravel, revealing the incongruence between these beliefs and my evolving sense of self. The struggle to break free from these confines was palpable, yet with each written word, I chipped away at the stains of judgment, paving the way for a more authentic exploration of love and intimacy. This narrative, marked by inner conflict and self-discovery, serves as a testament to the on-going journey of liberation from fossilised beliefs, striving to embrace the fullness of my authentic self.

Delving into the recesses of my consciousness, I uncover intricate layers surrounding the perceptions of physical intimacy and the act of making love, both inexplicably tethered to societal taboos, especially for women. As I embark on this journey of self-discovery, I immerse myself in introspection, pouring my reflections onto paper, engaging in profound meditation, and contemplating the deeply ingrained beliefs that have shaped my view of these experiences. The realisation strikes that these beliefs are not truly mine; they are borrowed shackles that do not serve my genuine desires.

Shedding the weight of these societal impositions, I come to a profound understanding of physical intimacy as a beautiful dance, a tango between two souls and bodies, resonating with infinite joy. What I glean from this revelation is obscured by the negative filters imposed by external influences. I acknowledge the beauty and richness of this human connection, a truth obscured for far too long during my married life when I was conditioned to view such expressions as clandestine and shameful. However, as I confront the fossilised beliefs at their roots, a transformative process unfolds, urging me to decouple from the imposed judgments.

It is an arduous journey, not an instant metamorphosis. Yet, as I systematically chip away at these long-held convictions, the liberation is palpable. The freedom to relish the beauty of intimate connections, driven by mutual consent and adult agency, becomes a beacon guiding me out of the shadows of societal dogma. The process is on-going, marked by continuous reflection and contemplation, for these beliefs run deep and have been etched into my psyche over many years. Nevertheless, with each passing day, I reclaim more of my authentic self, savouring the tangled dance of bodies, and allowing fleeting thoughts to dissipate like wisps of clouds.

To confront fossilised beliefs, a critical initial step involves reflecting upon them. This reflective process is paramount for anyone traversing the path of self-improvement and striving for personal evolution. The journey towards greatness necessitates a deliberate effort to identify and dispel beliefs that no longer serve our growth. This endeavour begins with cultivating awareness—acknowledging the presence of these fossilised beliefs within our psyche.

Unearthing these deeply embedded convictions demands a nuanced approach. Fossilised beliefs, often ingrained since childhood, originate from a myriad of sources such as parental influence, societal norms, educational systems, and sometimes religious or cultural doctrines. These beliefs, occasionally gender-specific, reside in our subconscious, requiring us to delve into the roots of our psyche. Patience becomes a virtue, for dismantling these long-standing beliefs is a gradual process, demanding compassion and understanding.

As we embark on the excavation of our beliefs, it is essential to illuminate their origins, recognising that they were not consciously chosen or planted by our own volition. This illumination creates a space for healing and provides an opportunity for intentional unlearning. However, it is crucial to navigate this terrain with empathy and kindness, as this exploration may uncover past traumas and discomfort. Healing, self-improvement, and the journey towards the desired self are not swift endeavours; they demand time, compassion, and a steadfast commitment to self-discovery.

While the process may be arduous, the dividends are immeasurable. Imagining personal growth as a perpetual process rather than a fixed destination aligns more cohesively with the fluidity of our evolving selves. This mental shift fosters a more sustainable and gratifying journey, emphasising that the continuous pursuit of improvement is, in itself, a destination worth pursuing.

Inescapably, every society, culture, family, parent, and teacher has played a role in shaping a child's life, often leaving indelible marks in diverse ways. This is an inherent aspect of human existence—a collective outcome of limited knowledge and awareness accessible to each individual, coupled with the depth of their understanding. Acknowledging this fact becomes the starting point for the journey of unlearning and de-fossilising beliefs that hinder personal growth.

Once the proverbial torch is shone on a fossilised belief, revealing its roots, the imperative next step is forgiveness. Regardless of whether the source is a person, a cultural norm, or an institutional belief system, holding onto grudges or assigning blame proves unproductive. Forgiveness becomes the key, a deliberate choice to release the hold of past influences and open the door to a more empowered future. The process involves a conscious decision-making juncture where one can choose to eradicate the belief entirely or modify and realign it with a more constructive perspective.

The critical juncture in this transformative process lies in taking responsibility for the chosen belief. As an adult armed with enhanced knowledge and awareness, consciously seeding a belief into the subconscious and conscious mind marks a pivotal moment. This acknowledgment is vital, as it positions the individual as the new source of influence. Understanding this responsibility underscores the agency one holds over the beliefs that shape their perception of self and the world. This intentional act of claiming ownership paves the way for a self-directed and empowered narrative, fostering personal growth and resilience in the face of ingrained beliefs.

Allow me to emphasise the steps once more, acknowledging the significance of awareness and knowledge in this transformative process. The journey begins with a heightened awareness, recognising the presence of fossilised beliefs that no longer contribute positively to our lives. Reflection on these beliefs becomes the key, delving into their origins and understanding that they were not consciously chosen but rather inherited from external sources.

As we shine a light on these beliefs and acknowledge their external origin, a crucial step follows—forgiving the source. Understanding that those who instilled these beliefs had limited knowledge and awareness at the time allows us to release the grip of resentment. This act of forgiveness is liberating, paving the way for conscious decision-making.

The subsequent step involves letting go and consciously choosing to replace or modify the belief. This is a moment of empowerment where we decide the narrative that will shape our perception of self and the world. Whether we opt for an entirely new belief or make subtle adjustments, the key is to align it with our present values and the future we envision.

Finally, and perhaps most significantly, we assume full responsibility for the new belief we have consciously selected. This responsibility signifies a shift in narrative control—from external influences to our own intentional choices. By taking ownership of our beliefs, we ensure that they serve the evolving version of ourselves, aligning with the aspirations we hold for the future.

It is crucial to acknowledge that the process of unlearning fossilised beliefs is time-consuming, requiring patience and self-compassion at each step. Whenever the journey feels overwhelming or painful, granting yourself a rest is a valid and necessary choice. Importantly, the goal in this transformative process is not to dwell excessively on the negatives of the past but to comprehend the origins of the fossilised beliefs. Through forgiveness, letting go, and intentional replacement with a new belief, the focus remains on moving forward.

The emphasis is on avoiding becoming entangled in the past, getting lost in a maze of negatives. The purpose is to understand, forgive, release, and then firmly replace the old belief with a new, constructive one. Life is an on-going journey, and the intention is to navigate it with a focus on the present and the days ahead. Caution is advised to prevent getting stuck in a past that hinders the ability to embrace the present and future fully. The key is to follow the steps, adopt a new belief, and persist with it until it becomes the dominant conscious choice, thereby replacing the outdated belief that no longer serves your personal growth.

The Crucial Influence of Your Environment

When we often discuss personal growth and development, it is easy to get lost in the individual's journey—their responsibilities, their awareness, their pursuit of knowledge, their unwavering persistence, and their deliberate actions to inch closer to their dreams and desires. Invariably, this narrative revolves around the individual—the person who makes decisions, crafts meticulous plans, and takes those deliberate, albeit sometimes timid, steps towards personal realisation.

Yet, it is imperative to delve deeper into the realm of transformation and explore an often underappreciated facet: the environment. You might refer to it as the context, the surroundings, or even the backdrop against which your life unfolds. However, for our purposes, 'environment' serves as the appropriate term, encompassing all these nuances. It includes the cultural milieu you immerse yourself in, the company you keep, the books you devour, the clubs and societies you belong to, and even the media channels you tune into.

In our youth, we are not typically afforded much choice in shaping our environment. It is often pre-determined, handpicked by our parents, society and school and unfolds organically. However, as we transition into adulthood, embarking on our journey of awareness, it is paramount that we take responsibility for the environment we expose ourselves to. It becomes our prerogative to carefully curate our surroundings, selecting our circles of friends, choosing the clubs and societies we partake in, opting for reading material that nourishes our minds, curating our TV channels, and consciously filtering the messages we encounter.

Now, let's peel back the layers to explore the dynamic influence of the environment through examples.

Contrasting Scenarios of Commitment

Let's paint two distinct scenarios to underscore the substantial impact of one's environment on their commitment to a newfound goal.

Scenario One: In the first scenario, envision an individual who resolves to wake up an hour earlier each day to embark on a 30-minute morning run. As we peer into their surroundings, we find a friend circle that largely disregards physical and mental well-being. Among their colleagues, only a scant few display an inclination for an active lifestyle. Our protagonist, upon returning home, embraces a penchant for unwinding in front of the television. This daily run commitment remains more of an idea, having been executed just once, dangling in limbo—undefined.

Scenario Two: Now, shift your focus to the second scenario, which unfolds quite differently. Here, a determined individual charts a course to rise an hour ahead of their usual time, ensuring a dedicated 30-minute morning run. They have etched this goal in ink, mapping out a strategy that entails retiring an hour earlier each night. Yet, it does not stop there. This person collaborates with a nearby friend, forging a mutual commitment and designing a shared plan. Should either falter in motivation on a given day, the fail-safe strategy activates: a gentle nudge or a friendly knock on the door. This pact is not merely verbal; it is inked into a written agreement, a binding contract that both parties wholeheartedly endorse. Their pact extends beyond short-term aspirations. In a show of unwavering determination, they set their sights on a half marathon for the coming year. Every detail is meticulously documented, and these two friends double as colleagues, offering a support system intertwined with their daily routines. Together, they not only adhere to their plan but also fuel each other's enthusiasm, amplifying their shared journey with positivity.

These scenarios serve as a testament to the monumental role that one's environment plays in shaping their commitment. It is not merely about individual aspiration; it is a collaborative dance between personal drive and the world that surrounds us.

Let's delve deeper into these two scenarios, dissecting the nuances that differentiate mere aspiration from a blueprint for success and the environment we choose to surround ourselves with.

Scenario One: In the initial scenario, we encounter a dream, and a desire, but therein lies a critical absence—a well-defined plan. What remains shrouded in uncertainty is the process leading up to the desired one-hour-earlier wake-up time. This person, in scenario one, acknowledges their wish, and their yearning, but lacks a vital support system. Their existence is steeped in other habits that lean more towards sedentary tendencies. It is a situation teetering on the brink of inaction.

Scenario Two: As we pivot to the second scenario, the landscape shifts remarkably. Here, our protagonist is not merely dreaming; they are thinking strategically, and discerningly. They commit to hitting the sack an hour earlier, thus surmounting a crucial hurdle. This individual proceeds to establish an unambiguous six-month plan—a plan bolstered by collaboration with a close friend and colleague. In this scenario, the person is already on a trajectory to success. The commitment is not vague or undefined; it boasts clarity. Moreover, it is not confined to just one aspect. In the wake of their six-month challenge, they set their sights on a half marathon for the upcoming year.

By meticulously outlining their steps and securing a companion for this journey, they build a robust foundation for success. Here, the power of the environment comes into stark focus. The choice to envelop oneself in a supportive, strategic, and encouraging setting—marked by both friends and colleagues—can lead to a cascade of positive changes. In the second scenario, the commitment is not isolated; it has the potential to permeate and transform multiple facets of one's life.

In conclusion, it is clear that our environment and the meticulous construction of a clear, actionable plan are potent catalysts for steering us towards our desired destinations. The second scenario, rich with a strategic approach and unwavering support, exemplifies the transformational potential of making the right choices in our surroundings.

Curating Your Life's Ecosystem

When I talk about 'environment,' I'm referring to the various forms of influences that envelop our lives. It encompasses the people you engage with, the groups you associate with, the resources at your disposal, the media you consume, the audio-visuals that shape your perceptions, the friends you hold close, the experts you seek counsel from, and the messages that subtly mould your thoughts. It is the intricate web of stimuli that colours your world.

From a certain juncture in life, every adult shoulders the responsibility of conscientiously, judiciously, and strategically selecting this environment. The choice hinges on creating a context in alignment with your envisioned future self—a future where your dreams materialise. This pivot towards a purposeful environment unfolds as a part of your self-awareness and conscious growth journey.

A pivotal aspect of crafting this supportive environment is the clarity that accompanies it. Once your intentions are committed to paper, a crystal-clear, precise roadmap emerges. Every line in your written plan becomes a beacon, illuminating the way forward.

As you can observe, each element seamlessly converges to pave a path that can usher you towards your dreams. The overarching message here is unmistakable: take ownership of your environment selection. Do it thoughtfully, do it consciously, do it wisely, and do it strategically. This proactive curation of your surroundings will render your journey towards realising your dreams smoother and more attainable.

In sum, the essential takeaway from this exploration is the empowering call to action—take responsibility for your life's ecosystem. Through careful, intentional, and strategic choices, you can fortify the scaffolding that supports your aspirations, making the path to your dreams far more navigable. And I am sure you have heard the famous saying that, *You are the sum of the five people that you surround yourself with*. So, choose those five people wisely; choose your environment, strategically.

The Unshakeable Power of Discipline

Welcome to a world where dreams materialise and your journey is an exhilarating expedition. The key to unlocking this realm? None other than the steadfast force of discipline.

Imagine you are standing at the threshold of transformation. You hold knowledge like a potent elixir, and your awareness shines like a guiding star. But here is the pivotal twist—the real magic, the true driver of transformation, is discipline. It is the unwavering bridge between desire and reality.

Let's get down to business. You have got the know-how, the awareness is humming, and you are geared up for action. But remember, knowledge in its purest form (i.e., raw knowledge) is not enough. Action is the secret sauce. And not just any action—consistent, dedicated, relentless action.

Discipline is your north star, your guiding light. It is your commitment to achieving the improbable, the pledge to persevere when the path gets rugged. Picture your aspirations and cast them in stone—write them down, imbuing your dreams with tangible form. Lose 10 kilograms, double your income, enlarge your social circle; inscribe it all. There is magic in writing. Name your date with destiny, and then reverse engineer the journey. The step-by-step path you create becomes your blueprint, and discipline is your unwavering guide.

But here is a nugget of wisdom: focus on quantity before quality. Do not jump into the deep end of the pool; wade into your goals with a mere five-minute daily commitment. Start simple and watch how your discipline creates a bridge to quality. Over time, you will stretch the duration, intensify your efforts, and discover new dimensions of your potential.

We are all human, and let's face it, some days the couch beckons with irresistible allure. That is alright—embrace the humanity in you. Acknowledge the urge to procrastinate, but never surrender to it. Act first, and motivation will follow. The spark of action ignites the flame of motivation.

The power of discipline is your ultimate edge. It is the unwavering commitment to stride towards your goals, drowning out the distractions. It is your choice—will you be a dreamer or a doer? Those who choose discipline ascend the ladder of achievement, turning their aspirations into reality.

Remember, discipline is not a prison; it is the key to unlocking your potential. As we embark on this chapter, prepare to uncover the secrets of discipline, and to master the art of transcending excuses. We will equip you with the tools to dance in rhythm with your goals, to craft the masterpiece of your life through the unwavering cadence of discipline.

Secret Sauces

Having reflected on our habits, broken free from fossilised beliefs, conducted a spring cleaning, and fostered an environment conducive to cultivating the desired habits, coupled with unwavering discipline to actualise our goals and instil new habits, it is time to infuse some special sauces into this delectable feast of self-transformation. These sauces come in the form of playfulness, forgiveness, and gratitude.

Playfulness: The Joy of Fun in Adulting

As I embark on the daily journey of tasks and to-dos, a novel inquiry reverberates within me: How can I add intentional fun and playfulness into these routine activities? This contemplation, born out of a desire to infuse joy into the mundane, has become a guiding principle for me. A few months back, I made a conscious decision to inscribe 'fun' as a designated activity in my daily to-do list. Little did I anticipate the transformative impact this intentional injection of playfulness would have on my daily routine.

The act of turning the mundane into the extraordinary has become a delightful game, and each task is an opportunity to uncover creative ways to infuse joy. It is not merely about completing a checklist; it is about savouring the process, about finding the fun in the ordinary. This intentional playfulness has not only added a vibrant hue to my daily chores but has also ushered in a newfound enthusiasm. It is a gentle reminder that even in the midst of responsibilities, there is room for light-heartedness and a touch of whimsy. As I navigate through the landscape of my daily responsibilities, the intentional pursuit of fun has become a beacon, illuminating the path with a sense of play that transforms the ordinary into the extraordinary.

In the hustle and bustle of adult life, the essence of having fun seems to have slipped through the cracks, overshadowed by the weight of responsibilities and daily tasks. Unlike our carefree days of childhood when fun seamlessly intertwined with our activities, adulthood demands a conscious effort to infuse playfulness into our routine. This becomes especially crucial for tasks that do not inherently spark joy. Our responsibilities weave a complex web of everyday activities, and therein lies the challenge—how do we reintroduce the element of fun without turning everything into a monotonous military drill?

The call to intentionally inject fun and playfulness into our daily endeavours is not a plea to evade the challenges or shy away from daunting tasks. Instead, it is an invitation to approach them creatively, to step outside the conventional boundaries and view our responsibilities through a lens of innovation. By doing so, we not only achieve results but also transform the mundane into a playground of enjoyment. Embracing this mindset allows us to retain a sense of play reminiscent of our childhood, infusing our activities with a touch of the carefree spirit we once cherished.

Embarking on the journey of self-transformation is undoubtedly a serious endeavour, marked by challenges and the need to carve out new patterns in our lives. However, in the midst of this profound change, it becomes essential to intentionally infuse joy and revel in the process. Despite the inevitable hurdles and the call to break established norms, it does not mean the entire journey has to be devoid of fun or resemble a rigid, inflexible routine. On the contrary, to undertake this transformative path successfully, we must rekindle the artist within, awaken the dormant imagination, and unearth the child that still resides within us.

The childlike spirit, though possibly buried under the weight of responsibilities and daily tasks, is resilient and waiting to be rediscovered. It is a reminder that amidst the serious business of adulting, there exists an inner child eager to play. By intentionally incorporating elements of fun and playfulness into our daily activities and the overall process of self-transformation, we not only lighten the weight of the journey but also tap into the boundless creativity and joy that accompany our inner child. It is about giving that playful spirit a nod, allowing it to dance alongside us as we navigate the transformative path, proving that even in the most profound changes, joy can be a faithful companion.

When we think of change, awareness, and self-transformation, the immediate association often leans towards pain, rigidity, and hardship. While it is undeniable that the journey holds its share of challenges and the need to confront deep-seated issues, the key lies in recognising that it does not have to be needlessly painful. Pain is an inevitable aspect, involving the unravelling of traumas and the intricate process of healing. However, infusing elements of fun, and playfulness, and maintaining a light-hearted approach can serve as potent allies in navigating the difficulties that surface during this transformative journey.

Consider incorporating fun and playfulness as essential condiments, enriching your life, activities, and tasks. Just as one would sprinkle salt or pepper for flavour, add a touch of enjoyment to the process, regardless of the nature of the endeavour. Whether it is an intense gym session, launching a new business, or embarking on any adventure, infusing a bit of fun into the mix can prove transformative. At the end of the day, those who embrace more joy in their pursuits often emerge as the true winners, finding a balance between the serious and the light-hearted on the path to self-discovery.

Forgiveness

The days were slowly but surely unfolding in Sydney, as I familiarised myself with the local supermarket and my dormitory-like residence nestled within a monastery. Among my fellow residents, predominantly university students, I was finding my footing in the vibrant rhythm of life down under. My pursuit of a PhD scholarship had culminated in my arrival in this distant land, and the excitement that had ignited my journey had not dimmed; if anything, it had grown brighter with each passing day.

As the clock neared 8 p.m., I found myself on my single bed, my sanctuary in this bustling city. My phone suddenly chimed, breaking the tranquil evening. I glanced at the message, and there it was—a message from my ex-husband, someone with whom I had shared the tumultuous end of a marriage without any closure. His simple greeting, 'Hi, how are you?' stared back at me from the screen.

I hesitated, contemplating whether to respond. I had resolved to move forward, to let go of the past and embrace my newfound journey of healing and self-discovery. I knew deep down that this was not the moment for closure, not with the wounds still fresh. So, I made a conscious choice not to reply. However, within moments, another message followed a reminder of my own words, 'Can't we still be friends, even if we divorce?'

Yes, it was me who had said those very words, trying to navigate the complexities of our relationship as it crumbled. Yet, I realised that words could hold different meanings at different times, and this message had the potential to unravel the peace I had fought so hard to attain.

In that crucial moment, I made a decision, not borne out of anger or revenge but from a place of self-respect and a yearning to protect the hard-won tranquillity I had found in my new life. I chose not to respond. Instead, I embarked on a grander path, one of forgiveness—both for him and for myself.

This was not a way to hold onto the past; it was my bridge to the future, my essential step towards healing and transformation. So, I forgave him, and each time his memory surfaces, I send him nothing but love and well wishes, hoping he is living a fulfilling life, just as I am determined to do. Forgiveness became an integral part of my journey, an act of self-preservation, and a testament to my newfound strength and healing.

Forgiveness, in my view, stands as a cornerstone of self-transformation and healing, an integral component of a conscious and self-aware individual. It extends beyond pardoning others for perceived or actual wrongs; it encompasses forgiving ourselves. This belief is rooted in several compelling reasons, a few of which I would like to delve into.

Firstly, every decision we make, including those involving others, is shaped by the knowledge, awareness, and resources available to us at a specific point in time. These factors are perpetually incomplete and evolving. Consequently, actions that we or others take may be misinterpreted as unjust or wrong based on the information and awareness we possess at that moment. Recognising this grants us the power to either extend forgiveness to ourselves for our past decisions and actions or to forgive others for their actions, driven by their limited knowledge and information at that particular time.

This perspective is not only logical but also a hallmark of an individual who has attained a heightened level of self-awareness. It underscores the fallibility inherent in all humans and the limitations we face when it comes to information and knowledge. Embracing this awareness is the first step towards forgiveness, both of ourselves and of others, leading to personal growth and healing.

Another compelling reason to emphasise the significance of forgiveness lies in the power of liberation that it grants. When we extend forgiveness, whether to others or ourselves, we release the mental and emotional burden of dwelling on past grievances. This act of letting go bestows upon us the invaluable gifts of time and energy, which we might otherwise squander on rumination, analysis, self-critique, or harbouring resentment. Instead, we can channel these precious resources towards constructive self-improvement and personal growth.

In essence, forgiveness enables us to redirect the time and energy we would have expended on the past towards the present moment, which serves as a foundational building block for our future selves. This redirection is a logical concept, but it demands a heightened level of awareness and understanding to be fully appreciated. It requires us to recognise the inherent value of our limited, precious time and energy, the currency of each 24-hour cycle. Each morning we open our eyes, it is akin to a rebirth, a fresh opportunity to make the most of the day. Wasting this invaluable chance on blame or resentment seems counterproductive when we could instead invest it in actions that yield present and future benefits. Hence, the second compelling reason that underscores the power of forgiveness is the ability to save time and energy and to use them wisely and productively, benefiting not just today but also tomorrow and the days to come.

Another remarkable facet of forgiveness lies in the profound emotional relief it can bestow upon us when we embark on the path of self-forgiveness and forgiving others for perceived or actual wrongs. Picture this as a gradual process of shedding the emotional baggage we have been carrying. In this metaphorical scenario, envision a backpack laden with stones, each stone representing an unforgiven aspect of yourself or a transgression by others.

As you journey through life, healing, evolving, and transforming towards your desired self, with every act of self-forgiveness and forgiving others, one of these heavy stones is cast away. With each stone's removal, your burden becomes lighter. Imagine the passage of time and the diminishing number of stones in your backpack. Picture how much lighter, agile, focused, and energised you will become in your life's journey, the most significant journey of all.

This life is a precious gift, and we bear the responsibility to make the most of it based on the knowledge, information, and awareness available to us. I offer you this vivid imagery to illustrate how forgiveness can gradually unburden you as you journey through life. Envision the day when you can finally set the entire backpack down. While it's a gradual process that takes time, it is entirely possible. Consider that day and practice letting go—forgive yourself, your parents, your former partners, and your friends, and most importantly, forgive yourself to become your own best friend in this beautiful journey of life.

It is vital to clarify that when discussing the concept of forgiveness, I am referring to an internal process within yourself—your thoughts, judgments, and your inner psychological and emotional world. I am by no means suggesting that you should grant people who have wronged you second or third chances to repeat their transgressions. What I mean by forgiveness is primarily for your own well-being. It is about finding inner peace and freeing up time and energy to focus on aspects of your life that empower you and help you thrive.

Setting boundaries is a significant part of this process. You must establish boundaries with individuals who bring negativity into your life, those who drain your energy, and those who hinder your journey to success. Distinguishing between forgiveness as an inner transformation and allowing repeated harm from external sources is crucial. Everything I discuss regarding forgiveness occurs within your own thoughts, mind, and consciousness.

This concept of forgiveness is closely related to the importance of setting boundaries for yourself. It revolves around self-respect, self-love, the company you keep, the companions you allow into your life, and the groups or circles you associate with. When you forgive, it is an act of self-love, an affirmation of your self-worth, and a declaration that you deserve peace. You understand that the time and energy spent on not forgiving and dwelling on past events can be better invested in yourself, leading to a lighter heart and greater peace of mind. If you feel that forgiving someone might allow them to hurt you again, rest assured that you are in control, and you have the power to decide. For instance, I chose not to respond to my ex-husband's message when I arrived in Sydney, because I wanted not to engage in further drama, and because I respected and valued myself. I forgave, and that act of forgiveness occurred within me, bringing me peace and clarity.

Gratitude: A Daily Celebration of Life's Treasures

Each day, I engage in an important ritual, a cherished practice that centres me and fills me with an overwhelming sense of gratitude for the myriad of experiences woven throughout my life. With unwavering devotion, I dedicate time to acknowledge and celebrate my existence, the knowledge that courses through my veins, and the incredible journey I have embarked upon. This ritual is my daily sanctuary of gratitude, a time to count my blessings and to reflect upon my path.

My gratitude journey unfolds with the creation of ever-expanding lists of achievements, milestones, and moments of triumph that have shaped my life. The fruits of my gratitude are neatly housed within a special repository, my cherished gratitude box. This vessel holds not just words, but fragments of my journey, each inscribed with moments of victory, dreams realised, and experiences that have painted my life with vibrant hues. On those days when shadows loom large, I turn to this treasure trove of achievements. As I sift through the contents, I am reminded of the long and arduous path I have journeyed thus far, the hurdles I have leaped, and the resilience that courses through my veins. It is in these moments that I gently reassure myself that it is perfectly human to feel down at times, but it is an opportunity to place my hand upon my heart, take a deep breath, and rise once more to stride towards my dreams, to evolve, and to embrace the challenges that lie ahead.

Gratitude and acknowledgement are not mere tokens in my life; they are the heartbeat of my daily existence. These expressions of thankfulness extend beyond the grand accomplishments to embrace life's simplest gifts, like the sun's morning caress and the whimsical dance of a butterfly in the embrace of spring. They reach their crescendo in monumental achievements like securing a cherished job, witnessing my first book grace the world, or receiving the cherished visa that united me with family in Australia. It is this practice, this skill, this art of gratitude that I firmly believe every individual should not only learn but diligently cultivate and nurture each day of their lives. For it is in the essence of gratitude that we uncover the secret to savouring life's most profound joys and navigating its most profound challenges.

Think back to the last time someone's kindness graced your life, enveloping you in a comforting, almost magical warmth. It is in those moments of altruism when we experience emotions that elevate our spirits, filling us with an overwhelming sense of gratitude and appreciation. That act of kindness, a gift from another in the midst of their own bustling existence, creates an exquisite mix of emotions. Whenever we recall these moments, the warmth of gratitude resurfaces, reminding us of the generosity and goodwill of others. This warmth, a sensation that courses through our bodies, is where gratitude draws its profound power.

Emotions are a force to be reckoned with, and gratitude leverages its potency by weaving itself into this tapestry of feelings. It is this interweaving, this connection between gratitude and the sensation of warmth and homeliness that underscores the significance of gratitude in our lives. To tap into this power, we must consciously recognise, appreciate, and express gratitude for our journey thus far. Beyond celebrating our achievements and successes, we must also embrace the mundane yet profound aspects of existence. We should be grateful for the gift of life, for every breath that sustains us, and for the blessing of good health. Let us express gratitude for the 24 hours that dawn anew each day as we open our eyes, for our strength and youth, and for the precious, healthy limbs that grant us mobility. Our gratitude extends to the incredible people who grace our lives and the countless opportunities and resources that present themselves. Even during challenging moments, when life may not align with our desires or expectations, we can appreciate the lessons that adversity offers. It becomes a signal to release the people or habits that no longer serve our well-being, as gratitude guides us to the path of self-improvement and growth. What I wish to emphasise is that, each day, countless opportunities emerge for us to express gratitude, to recognise our achievements, and to acknowledge our place in this beautiful journey.

In the journey of self-transformation, as we tread the path towards a more evolved, future version of ourselves, daily acknowledgements and expressions of gratitude serve as vital signposts. However, possessing the skill of gratitude and an awareness of the countless blessings in our lives requires a substantial level of consciousness, maturity, and personal growth. It is not a terrain traversed by all, and that is why we often encounter individuals who seem bereft of gratitude. Their absence of appreciation stems from the fact that not everyone has reached, or ever will reach, the profound level of awareness and depth necessary to be thankful to the universe and to themselves.

As we reflect on this profound journey of self-discovery, we understand that gratitude is more than just a polite gesture; it is a manifestation of inner growth and self-awareness. It is a conscious recognition of the hurdles surmounted, the obstacles overcome, and the unwavering resilience displayed in the face of life's challenges. It is a celebration of the burning passion for our desires and the relentless pursuit of our loftiest goals. The depth of gratitude reflects the depth of our own being, and not everyone has delved into these depths. This realisation invites us to embrace our own growth and personal evolution while also extending compassion to those who may not have reached the same level of awareness. It is a reminder that each person's journey is unique, and their path towards gratitude is a personal expedition worth celebrating.

One of the most transformative and enriching rituals you can embrace in your life is keeping a gratitude journal. This journal serves as your sanctuary of appreciation, where you pen down your achievements, your blessings, and your thanks for all aspects of life, no matter how seemingly small or inconsequential. The act of scribbling down your gratitude, even as trivial as the morning sunlight or the first sip of coffee, carries immeasurable significance. These moments, humble though they may appear, are the building blocks of a life filled with thankfulness. Their scale and significance pale before the wireless and expansive power of gratitude.

When you commit to this daily practice, an extraordinary transformation unfurls. The energy of gratitude, as it permeates your life, begins to attract more opportunities, people, and moments for which you can be grateful. It becomes a positive feedback loop, where your expressions of appreciation lead to more appreciation from the world around you. The profound ripple effect of your gratitude becomes evident as you accumulate an ever-growing bank of acknowledgments and thanks. Each time you revisit your gratitude journal or sift through the notes in your gratitude box in the years to come, you will find a reservoir of gratitude that continues to deepen and expand. This inexhaustible wellspring of appreciation nurtures more successes and draws in more opportunities, reinforcing the cycle of gratitude. As your life unfolds, it is these small acts of gratitude that illuminate your path and remind you of the transformative journey of self-evolution you have embarked upon.

Summary: Unveiling the Steps to Evolve Yourself

Embarking on the transformative journey of evolving the self begins with a profound 'Why.' Delve into the depths of your motivations, and you will discover a powerful force—it is the love and respect you hold for yourself, recognising your inherent worth. As you acknowledge your potential and the limitations of your current knowledge, understand that you are not rooted like a tree; you have the capacity to grow and change.

Fuel your journey with curiosity and imagination. Write your statement of purpose, whether it is for the short-term, medium-term, or long-term. At this juncture, fears may surface as hesitant shadows. Embrace the ever-present uncertainty of life, cultivating the mental toughness needed for resilience.

Take a close look at your habits and life. Reflect, break free from past fossilised beliefs, and spring clean those that no longer serve you. Through reflection, learning, and conscious choices, navigate the influence of your environment—consider the people, resources, groups, energies, and influences around you.

In the realm of habits, employ the unshakeable power of discipline. Choose to change, replace, or improve habits and beliefs that no longer serve your evolution. The decisions are yours to make. Now, introduce the secret sauces of self-transformation: playfulness, forgiveness, and gratitude. Enjoy the process, forgive those who may have caused harm or planted limiting beliefs in your mind, and be grateful for what you have achieved, including holding and reading this book.

Imagine this process as preparing a delicious meal. You have put it on the stove, but remember transformation takes time. Let it simmer, exercise patience, and continue to act with discipline, persistence, and perseverance. Congratulations! You've initiated your journey of self-transformation and evolution. Welcome to the path.

What follows is a simple visual representation of these steps to guide you on your evolving journey.

1. **Step 1: Start with Why: Why Self-Transformation?**
   o 'Ask Yourself: Why embark on this journey?'
2. **Step 2: Self-Love and Respect**
   o 'Because you love and respect yourself.'
3. **Step 3: Acknowledge Your Potential and Limited Knowledge**
   o 'Acknowledge your oceanic potential and limited knowledge.'
4. **Step 4: Curiosity and Imagination**
   o 'Be curious, use your imagination, and write your statement of purpose.'
5. **Step 5: Embrace Uncertainty**
   o 'Embrace uncertainty, cultivate mental toughness.'
6. **Step 6: Reflect on Habits**
'Reflect on your habits/beliefs; break free from fossilised beliefs/habits.'
7. **Step 7: Environment and Discipline**
   o 'Acknowledge your environment, use unshakeable discipline'
8. **Step 8: Secret Sauces**
   o 'Playfulness, Forgiveness, Gratitude'
9. **Step 9: Simmer and Patience**
   o 'Let it simmer, be patient, act with discipline and persistence'
10. **Step 10: Congratulations!**
   o 'Congratulations! Welcome to the self-transformation path.'

Chapter Six
Bonuses

Passing the Torch of Knowledge: A Tale of Responsibility

After embarking on this lifelong journey of self-transformation, as you continuously evolve and strive to become better versions of yourself, it is essential to acknowledge that the process is on-going. We can establish short-term, medium-term, and long-term goals, focusing on various aspects of our lives when crafting our statements of purpose. As we progress through these steps and witness the enhancement in the quality of our lives—experiencing increased fulfilment, gratitude, satisfaction, and happiness—it becomes our responsibility to pass on the torch.

In my journey through life, the profound impact of knowledge has been undeniable. It is not just the acquisition of knowledge that has shaped me, but the deep-seated belief in the responsibility that comes with it. This sense of responsibility, the duty to share, to enlighten, has been a driving force in my life. It is one of the core reasons why I felt compelled to pen this book.

From the very inception of this endeavour, I envisioned a simple yet powerful goal: if this book could alter the life or perspective of just one person, it would have served its purpose magnificently. Knowledge carries the weight of responsibility with it, and I am determined to emphasise the transformative potential that lies within awareness and the action it begets.

We live in a world where knowledge is a dynamic, ever-evolving entity. It is not static; it is fluid, shaped by the hands that carry it forward. Knowledge, if left stagnant, becomes stagnant itself. It is akin to still water that stagnates over time. To breathe life into it, we must take action, build upon it, and pass it on, enriched and fortified.

Writing this book serves as my conduit to share the knowledge that life has bestowed upon me through various channels—books, experiences, people, and contemplation. Through the prism of my own life, I want to convey the essence of this responsibility that accompanies knowledge.

For me, this sense of duty began early, perhaps as far back as my first-grade classroom. I always yearned to be the teacher's assistant, eager to impart understanding to my peers who were grappling with their studies. This role followed me throughout my educational journey. The joy of sharing, of illuminating others' paths with knowledge, has always been a defining aspect of my identity.

I can now see that this responsibility is deeply woven into the tapestry of my being, nurtured both by my upbringing in an academic environment and the intrinsic calling I felt within. It is a beautiful amalgamation of nature and nurture.

Writing this book is my way of leaving a legacy, a tangible record of my lifelong commitment to this responsibility. If I have lived a life in accordance with my values and the sense of responsibility that comes with them, this book is the testament.

But, dear reader, the journey does not end here. In the pages that follow, should you discover even a glimmer of wisdom or a spark of insight, remember that the mantle of responsibility passes on to you. It is your duty to share that knowledge, to enrich it, and to impact at least one life in a positive way.

What follows in the following pages are some simple, yet practical steps to improve your life.

Simple Practical Steps to Improve Your Life

Unlock the Power of Your Posture: In the intricate dance of life, the way we stand and move plays a pivotal role. Our posture, a silent narrator of our inner world, can shape our feelings, perceptions, and reactions. It is a reflection of our essence, the visible echo of our presence.

So, let's delve into the art of self-improvement, one practical step at a time. Start by honing your posture—stand tall, with the grace of a triumphant oak, and sit with the poise of a sage contemplating the cosmos. A simple, yet profound shift. When you stand tall, your spirit soars; slouch and you invite the grumpier shadows of your soul.

In your quest for personal transformation, make this your starting point. Pay attention not only to your height but to the elegant alignment of your spine. Feel the earth beneath your feet, and let your weight be an even melody between both. It is in these subtleties that we discover the magic of presence.

Elevate your awareness of how you present your body in the theatre of life. Your posture is a story, and it is time to write a tale of strength, confidence, and transformation.

Unleash the Power of Your Mind: Within the intricate web of our inner thoughts lies a treasure trove of potential. Your mind is the canvas where linguistic awareness and inner dialogue come to life. Each thought is a brushstroke on this canvas, and it is time to paint a masterpiece.

Start with the simplicity of observation. Take a moment each day to witness the thoughts that flow through your mind like a river. Are they your allies, propelling you forward, or foes, holding you back? Explore their tone—are they nurturing or critical? Now, decide which thoughts are keepers and which are better replaced.

The words you choose in your thoughts matter. Do they uplift or weigh you down? The tone of your internal dialogue—is it gentle like a spring breeze or judgmental like an unforgiving critic? Each of these facets can be nurtured, refined, and developed as you embark on your journey of self-development and life transformation.

It won't always be a smooth path. At the start, it may feel like learning a new skill, a challenge to your mind's comfort zone. But remember, great things require effort. The prize for mastering the art of cultivating your thoughts is immeasurable. There is a rewarding transformation waiting for you at the end of this journey.

Simplify Your Surroundings: In the chaos of the modern world, an age-old wisdom beckons us to embrace simplicity. Minimalism, a timeless concept championed by various religions and philosophies, promises a path to peace of mind. Yet, it stands in stark contrast to the relentless consumerism of our twenty-first century existence, where we are bombarded with messages urging us to acquire, hoard, and accumulate.

The pressure to amass possessions is intertwined with our sense of identity and self-worth. But consider this: the fewer possessions we have, the less time and energy we need to devote to their care. It is a simple equation—fewer things, less effort.

Whether you are caught in the throes of consumerism, treading the path of minimalism, or have already embraced simplicity, decluttering your environment is a powerful step towards self-improvement and transformation. Much like the age-old tradition of spring cleaning in cultures worldwide, we need a system.

It could be a monthly ritual, a seasonal cleanse, or an annual purge depending on your pace. When time is tight, start with your workspace, your sanctuary of productivity. Go through each item, and if it is unnecessary, consider donating, up cycling, or finding a new purpose for it. Categorise and conquer, and you will find that a clutter-free workspace not only eases your daily tasks but also paves the way for peace of mind.

The truth is we do not need most of the possessions that fill our lives. This applies to our closets, kitchen utensils, electronic gadgets, and more. Periodically, take stock and declutter. Embrace a system of sharing, swapping, upcycling, and recycling. By simplifying your environment, you will not only transform your surroundings but also cultivate habits that align with your best self.

In the battle between a cluttered, chaotic space and a serene, minimalist haven, the latter often emerges as the catalyst for profound change.

Shed the Weight of Judgment: In our journey of self-improvement and life enhancement, there exists a simple yet profound step—the reduction of judgment. This act, which encompasses self-judgement and judgement of others, is integral to our daily lives. Just as our minds teem with thousands of thoughts, so too does judgment form a natural part of each individual's mental landscape. We judge ourselves, those around us, our circumstances, our past, and our future.

Our tendency towards negativity bias further fuels this judgemental nature. However, recognising that this is part of our human wiring, we can consciously nurture a mindset of less judgement. Such a shift has the power to bestow upon us a newfound peace of mind, a path to self-development, and richer relationships both with ourselves and the world.

Reducing judgement closely aligns with observing the thoughts that flow through our minds. Once you identify a judgemental thought, you face a choice. Does it serve you? Is it productive? Is it worthy of your precious time and energy? If the answer is no, you can replace it with something positive—an affirmation for yourself, a kinder perspective of someone else, or a more constructive view of a situation.

Through diligent practice, just as with any habit, you will gradually cultivate the art of judgment reduction. The result? A mind with fewer intrusive thoughts, less judgement, and an elevated quality of thoughts and judgements. These are thoughts and judgments that are productive, useful, and genuinely deserving of your time and energy.

Set Boundaries: Setting boundaries, a cornerstone of self-love and self-respect, holds an indispensable place in every person's life. It is a practice that calls for safeguarding our personal space with diligence. It also demands that those around us are aware of these boundaries. It is a shared responsibility, as individuals, to not only establish our own boundaries clearly but to also recognise and respect the boundaries of those we interact with daily. This kind of awareness and accountability can significantly impact our decisions and responses.

When we are in tune with our boundaries and have firmly established them, it becomes easier to decline invitations or extra work that does not align with our personal journey or our vision of the future self we aspire to be. Setting boundaries not only simplifies decision-making but also conserves our precious time and energy. It is about understanding the limits of our personal space, determining the behaviours we will accept or not, and defining the individuals we welcome into our lives.

It is essential to note that setting boundaries is not about confining ourselves; instead, it is a means of remaining in control of our lives. As we evolve, our boundaries can evolve with us. The choice to expand or maintain these boundaries is a reflection of our personal growth.

Honouring the Boundaries of Others: The practice of boundary setting is not a one-way street; it is a two-way interaction that hinges on respect. In addition to defining and safeguarding our personal boundaries, we also bear the responsibility of acknowledging and honouring the boundaries of others. This extends to every facet of our lives, particularly with individuals we have frequent and continuous interactions with.

To foster a climate of understanding and mutual respect, it is crucial to seek clarity when we encounter uncertainty regarding someone else's boundaries. This is especially significant when it comes to people we frequently engage with. By being attuned to their boundaries, we pave the way for respect, nurturing these limits while simultaneously conserving our own time and energy during interactions.

Setting boundaries is a dual commitment—one for ourselves and another in our interactions with others. It is a dynamic process that evolves as we grow, and the respect we extend to these boundaries likewise evolves in tandem.

Embrace Mindfulness: Mindfulness, a concept that has been making waves in recent times, is not just a passing trend. The reason behind the mindfulness hype is its profound impact. When we engage with life mindfully, we consciously participate in each facet of our existence. From the decisions we make to our interactions, from the words we choose to the thoughts we harbour, mindfulness brings a heightened level of awareness and intentionality to our actions.

This conscious awareness and mindfulness go hand in hand, functioning as inseparable allies. By infusing mindfulness into our daily routine, we pave the way for a more harmonious life. These are pivotal steps in the journey of self-development and life transformation. As we cultivate mindfulness in our lives, we elevate our overall quality of life, effectively propelling us towards a life that is not only improved but also truly transformed.

To me, mindfulness is the art of living consciously, deeply aware of how we navigate life, how we breathe, how we move, and how we connect with others. It extends to the very essence of our existence, from our simplest actions like eating or walking to more complex decisions about the company we keep. The beauty of mindfulness lies in its simplicity and versatility. Start small, take those initial steps, and watch as mindfulness ignites your life, spreading like wildfire, touching every corner of your existence.

Keep a Pen and Notebook Handy: I am an unwavering believer in the extraordinary power of writing. Whether you have a clear goal, a well-crafted plan, or a vision of the new, improved version of yourself that you are striving to become, it all needs to be put down on paper. There is magic in the act of writing, an alchemy that transforms mere thoughts into organised, tangible entities. When you jot down your thoughts and aspirations, you take the first step in turning them into concrete plans. Your desires and dreams shift from being vague wishes to well-defined, practical steps that propel you towards actual transformation.

That is why I advocate for keeping a trusty pen and notebook close at hand. While your phone can serve the purpose, I am a firm believer in the beauty of tangible, handwritten notes. Your ideas, your affirmations, and the phone numbers you want to call later—they all have a place on those pages. Whether your notebook rests next to your bed, resides in your bag, or takes pride of place on your office desk, always have it within arm's reach. Notes jotted down are like beacons of light, rescuing your fleeting thoughts from the clutches of forgetfulness. Once penned, ideas are never lost, and you can always refer back to them.

With each note you take and each plan you sketch out, you create a roadmap for your journey of transformation. As you build this collection of notes, it is like accumulating milestones of your progress. The sense of accomplishment you will experience is unlike any other, serving as fuel for your enthusiasm and motivation. You will find yourself not only more resolute in your journey but also brimming with the energy and determination to achieve even more—a sure-fire way to recharge your batteries and continue your path toward success.

Take Your Sleep Seriously: Let me underscore the profound importance of the quality of sleep in your daily life. It is vital to stress the 'daily' aspect here, as it is not possible to compensate for a week of disrupted sleep by indulging in a 12-hour slumber on the weekend. Our approach to sleep requires a serious upgrade—this is a fundamental pillar of self-improvement and life transformation.

Taking your sleep seriously involves a holistic perspective on your sleep environment and habits. It is not just about the number of hours you spend in slumber, which, for most adults, hovers around seven to eight hours. It encompasses every detail, from the bed you lie on, the mattress and pillow you rest your head upon, the room's temperature, and how dark it is. It is about the contents of your bedroom, whether you spend the hours before sleep plugged into electronic gadgets or engage in reading, mindfulness, or meditation practices.

I firmly advocate for being nestled in bed by 9:30 or 10 p.m. at the latest, with no screens in sight. This is your time to unwind, perhaps reading a few pages from the book on your nightstand, practising meditation or mindfulness, or engaging in a soothing pre-sleep ritual. Harness the power of positive thinking and gratitude to reflect on the day's efforts, all before 11 p.m. Your cool, almost pitch-dark bedroom will cradle you into a peaceful sleep, setting the stage for a spectacular day ahead.

If you are searching for a single, impactful step to elevate your life's quality and propel your transformation journey, then this is it—take your sleep seriously.

Embrace the Rhythmic Dance of Motion: Our bodies are exquisite creations, designed to be in perpetual motion. They rebel against a sedentary existence, and in this modern age, where many of us are tethered to computers for an average of eight hours a day, the discord is clear. We recognise the demands of our contemporary lifestyles, but we must also acknowledge our bodies' fundamental need to move.

So, how do we bridge this gap? The answer is simple: keep moving. The spectrum of movement is wide, from fidgeting, stretching, and walking to running, jumping, or even a spirited session of boxing. It can be as subtle as wiggling your fingers or your head during a virtual meeting, or a more pronounced sway of your hips. The possibilities are endless, and the benefits are boundless.

Embarking on your self-transformation journey can commence with a single, practical step—move more. Begin by infusing motion into your daily routine. Fidget while you work, and every 20 to 30 minutes rise from your chair to fetch a glass of water. Engage in a few stretches, perform a quick squat during a Zoom meeting, or sway your hands and feet. Stand and then sit back down. Any form of movement is not only beneficial but essential.

Movement is an intrinsic part of our humanity. While the configuration of our lives may have evolved with modernity, our biology remains resolute—we need to move. The beauty of it all is that you can choose the form of movement that resonates with you; there is no prescribed formula. Embrace the liberating joy of motion, for it is a simple yet profound step you can take right now to enrich your life. The best part? It is an open canvas for you to paint with the hues of your unique preferences and desires.

Elevate Your Nutrition: You have undoubtedly heard the adage, 'You are what you eat.' Let me assure you, it holds true. In our age, where consumerism reigns supreme, the same principles apply to nutrition. We find ourselves in an era of fast food, convenience meals, and frozen delicacies, riddled with additives and chemicals that our bodies were never designed to contend with.

As someone who is conscientious, as someone on the transformative journey of self-improvement, it becomes our duty to enhance our nutrition. We must take responsibility for what we fuel our bodies with, for this vessel is the sole companion we shall have until we bid adieu to planet Earth.

So, if you are here reading this, seeking a simple step to enrich your life, that step is to enhance your nutrition. To provide your body with the essential macronutrients and micronutrients, and to eschew fast food, processed fare, and frozen meals as much as possible. I say 'as much as possible' because I understand that everyone leads a busy life, and occasional indulgences are inevitable. We can allow for flexibility, but the primary focus should remain on what we ingest, for this body will be our lifelong companion.

It is our responsibility to undertake the requisite research to discern its needs and facilitate its thriving. We aspire to thrive with our bodies, to co-pilot our transformative life journeys. Consequently, we must supply the nutrition that aligns with the path we have chosen. Allow me to illustrate with an example: fruits. Fruits are undeniably wonderful, brimming with minerals and vitamins. However, they also contain sugar (fructose and glucose). The point here is that moderation is key for even good things must be consumed judiciously.

Practice Moderation: A pivotal facet of enhancing your nutrition is practising moderation by consuming less. Research on mice has revealed that when mice are given one-third of their usual diet, they enjoy longer lifespans. I am not suggesting that you drastically reduce your daily caloric intake to a third, but rather, aim to consistently eat slightly less in every meal and snack. You can start with a smaller plate to assist in this endeavour. It will require a degree of conscious effort and the formation of new habits, which can be challenging initially, but with time, it becomes a natural part of your routine.

Eating in moderation reduces the workload on your body when digesting food and converting it into energy. Your body will adjust, and you will find yourself content and satisfied with smaller portions. For instance, if you usually consume one whole apple daily, try reducing it to half an apple. If your lunch typically involves ten spoonful of rice, cut it down to seven. These are small, manageable steps to gradually consume less of what you are accustomed to.

Eating less can also involve timing your meals. Rather than eating whenever you please throughout the day, establish regular intervals, such as eating every two or three hours, allowing your body to rest during the intervals, creating mini-fasting periods. Another approach to eating less is intermittent fasting, a popular trend nowadays. In this method, you restrict your eating to a specific window, perhaps six to eight hours each day, fasting for the remaining hours. During the fasting period, you can consume water, coffee, or various types of tea, but no solid food. It is crucial, however, to avoid overcompensating by eating excessively during the allotted eating window. Mindfulness is key when practising moderation in your diet.

Connect with Mother Nature: One of the simplest and most profound steps to enhance your life is to forge a deeper connection with Mother Nature. Spend more time outdoors, soaking in the wonders of the natural world. Even if you do not have immediate access to the great outdoors, watching nature documentaries or simply gazing out of a window to appreciate the world outside can work wonders.

Take a leisurely stroll and pay close attention to the intricate petals of a flower, or observe the industrious ants labouring diligently. Inhale the sweet scent of a blooming blossom, or if you are fortunate enough to live near a forest, embark on a bushwalk. Hike to the top of a mountain, feel the refreshing spray of a waterfall, go for a jog, or rise early to witness a breathtaking sunrise. Visit the beach and watch the sun gracefully set, or marvel at the moon's majestic ascent. Allow the sand to tickle your toes and the ocean's embrace to wash over you. Experience the serenity of a camping trip, where the night's symphony is composed of chirping crickets. Lose yourself in the serene embrace of nature, or even hug a tree!

Mother Nature holds an abundance of wisdom and insight. She has mastered the art of perpetual self-improvement and transformation. We, as her children, can glean valuable lessons from her. We are intrinsically connected to nature and should endeavour to strengthen that bond. Observe how nature navigates the changing seasons, yet stands resolute and unwavering. Learn from the steadfastness of a tree, knowing that you, unlike a tree, have the power to transform yourself as you see fit.

If you seek a simple step to enrich your life, then reconnect with Mother Nature in any way that suits you. If direct access to nature is not available, you can still immerse yourself in its beauty through computer images and videos. Zoom in on a flower's delicate intricacies, and witness the splendour and complexity of the natural world.

Unplug from Your Devices: While technology has undoubtedly brought many benefits to our lives, it has also ensnared us in its grasp. Every day, we should allocate some hours to disconnect from our digital devices—be it our smartphones, laptops, or iPads. It is crucial to set them aside and step into the real world. Take a leisurely walk, delve into the pages of a physical book, engage in playful moments with your children, or simply take a well-deserved nap.

This act of detachment is absolutely vital. When you remove all technological distractions, you are left with yourself. It may lead to moments of boredom, but that very boredom can be a wellspring of creativity and introspection. It is where ideas are born, where self-discovery happens, and where you can delve into self-affirmations, introspection, and self-improvement.

This period of disconnection also offers quality time with your family and loved ones. So, one of the simplest yet most profound steps to enhance your life is to set aside your electronic gadgets for a few minutes to a few hours every day, depending on your circumstances. Do it and you will begin to notice the positive effects—how it aids you on your journey of life transformation. Embrace this habit of temporarily shelving your digital distractions.

Carry a Pocket-sized Companion: For those who know me, my passion for books is no secret. I firmly believe in the power of pocket-sized books as portable treasures. They can turn those pockets of idle time into opportunities for learning and personal growth. Whether you find yourself waiting in line, sitting in a coffee shop, or simply going about your daily life, these small books can be your constant companions.

Having a pocket-sized book with you is akin to keeping a pen and notebook handy at all times. When negative thoughts start to creep in, such as when you are waiting in line and find yourself silently judging the people around you, just reach for your pocket-sized book. Instead of indulging those negative thoughts or reflexively turning to your phone to check messages and emails, dive into the wisdom held within those pages.

Pocket-sized books are small wonders that can accompany you wherever you go. They are perfect for flights, train rides, car journeys, park outings, picnics, and more. They do not take up much space, but they hold immense potential for converting what might have been wasted time into moments of creativity and self-investment. With each page you read, you expand your knowledge and deepen your self-awareness.

This simple step is about having a pocket-sized companion that is always within reach. Of course, if electronic versions, audiobooks, or podcasts are more your style, then by all means, go for those. The key is to make learning and growth a continuous part of your life.

Swallow your frog at Dawn: In life and in our work, there are invariably tasks that we would rather avoid—those not-so-enjoyable responsibilities that can weigh us down. An essential step to enhance the quality of our lives is to tackle these tasks right at the beginning of our day, whether they pertain to work or our personal lives. By doing so, we 'swallow the frog' first thing in the morning.

This concept is inspired by the book 'Eat That Frog!' and it underscores the importance of handling the most vital, challenging, or unappealing aspects of your work or life that you might not particularly relish. When you 'swallow the frog' early in the day, it has a remarkable ripple effect on the hours that follow. Once you have conquered that challenging task, you will find yourself better equipped to approach the remainder of your day with enthusiasm and a sense of accomplishment.

The act of tackling your most challenging task in the morning provides you with a tangible sense of achievement and paves the way for a day filled with creativity and enjoyment. It leaves you feeling more joyful, more fulfilled, and ready to tackle the tasks that you genuinely relish. So, schedule your most demanding, least enjoyable task for the morning, 'swallow the frog,' and relish the benefits that follow.

Inject Intentional Fun and Playfulness into Your Life:
It is an unfortunate observation that for many adults, the joy of fun and playfulness tends to wane as they progress through adolescence and into adulthood. I firmly believe that we should proactively and deliberately infuse our lives with fun and playfulness in every possible way. Leaving it to chance is not an option. When I say 'intentionally' and 'strategically,' I mean we must make a conscious effort to bring fun and playfulness into our lives.

Having more fun is a vital aspect of winning in life. When I talk about having more fun, I do not mean evading difficult tasks, avoiding challenges, or taking the easy way out. Not at all. It is about making a list of the things you need to do daily or weekly and ensuring that even the most challenging tasks are included. Then, the next step is to consider how you can approach these tasks in a more playful and creative manner. In other words, you can tackle the tough stuff, step out of your comfort zone, and still have a great time. It is akin to hitting multiple birds with one stone.

I firmly believe that it is the responsibility of every individual to deliberately infuse fun and playfulness into every facet of their lives. By doing so, we can enter a state of flow where work no longer feels like work. Of course, there will still be moments when we have to 'swallow the frog,' and tackle hard and challenging tasks, and we can approach these with determination and seriousness. However, it does not mean we cannot have fun with the rest of our day, enjoy the process of self-improvement and self-transformation, and relish in the awareness and depth we gain in our lives. We are all winners in this playful and enjoyable journey of life.

Master the Art of Conscious Breathing: An essential concept closely tied to mindfulness is the practice of conscious breathing. Our breathing is something that is mostly automated; we do not consciously think about it or remember to do it because it is constantly happening. However, understanding that we have the power to intentionally change our breathing, to deliberately use our breath to feel calm and to transform our mood, holds incredible potential.

Recognising this power within our everyday, continuous process, we can use our breath to enhance our sense of calm, make better decisions, become more mindful, be fully present, and gain control over our thoughts, reducing judgement and heightening our awareness of our posture and tone of voice. Various breathing techniques are available for anyone to explore, but a straightforward step you can take at any moment during the day is to pause and shift from automatic to intentional breathing. Take a few moments to focus on your breath, repeating to yourself, 'I am breathing in, I am breathing out.' In less than a minute, you will find yourself feeling noticeably calmer and more composed. If you observe your thoughts after just a minute of deliberate, conscious breathing, you will notice that the whirlwind of thoughts has slowed down, providing you with a better chance to filter and assess the types of thoughts passing through your mind. You will also find that you are firmly grounded in the present moment, rather than dwelling on the past or rushing towards the future. One of the simplest steps to improve your life is to observe your breath, and calm yourself down, and, as I mentioned earlier, there are many other techniques to explore, but this is the easiest one to learn, use, and enjoy. Remember, you always have access to your breath and by focusing on it you can change your state of mind. What a powerful realisation.

Take Action and Transform Your Life

Having a list of simple, practical steps to improve your life and aid in your transformation journey is an excellent start. It is important to gather knowledge and raise awareness, but all that remains incomplete if you do not take action. Action is the bridge between knowledge and transformation. It is crucial to act, no matter how small the steps may seem, on the knowledge and awareness you have gained.

Chart your progress as you take action. Give yourself a timeframe to act upon these simple, practical steps. You need a clear start date and a finish date. Weekly reflections on your progress are beneficial. By setting a finish date, I do not mean that your journey ends; I mean that you should have a specific period, let's say three months, during which you focus on one aspect, like nutrition or eating moderately. Each week, reflect on how it went and what improvements can be made. After three months, look back and see how far you have come. If it has become a habit and a part of you, move on to the next practical step you want to integrate into your life.

To avoid overwhelming yourself, work on one aspect at a time. Choosing to tackle several aspects simultaneously can lead to either inaction or premature abandonment of your goals. Concentrate on one practical step, give yourself a month or two, work on it consistently, and then move on to the next when it feels like a habit.

As I always emphasise, keep a journal, create a chart, and hold yourself accountable. Take responsibility and be diligent. By taking action, reflecting, revising, and improving, you can systematically incorporate these simple, practical steps into your life.

If you work on one aspect each month for a year, you will become a transformed version of yourself compared to where you started at the beginning of that year. This transformation is a result of acting on your knowledge, not giving up too soon, being persistent, and maintaining discipline. Set aside time in your schedule to work on these habits, to journal and take notes, and to integrate these steps into your life.

Remember that transformation is an on-going process, much like the cycles of a year. You are continually improving, transforming, and evolving. You have got my support, and I wish you the best of luck. Happy practising, happy journaling, and happy reflecting as you act upon your newfound awareness. Keep shining on your journey of self-improvement and self-transformation.

Acknowledgements

In this section of the book, I wish to express my heartfelt gratitude to the individuals who have profoundly impacted my life's journey. The majority of these remarkable people are influential authors and renowned international speakers. It is imperative for me to recognise and extend my sincere appreciation to them, as their wisdom and insights have left an indelible mark on my life as I reflect on the experiences that have shaped me.

While it is impossible to acknowledge everyone, I hope to mention as many of them as I can, and I humbly apologise if I inadvertently omit someone.

The first person I wish to acknowledge is the incomparable Oprah Winfrey. I have further reserved a distinct section that follows this acknowledgement, specifically dedicated to Oprah Winfrey, which highlights the immense influence she has had on my perspective, self-confidence, and belief in my own potential. I have envisioned conversations with her, sitting on two chairs against a backdrop of lush greenery, discussing the very book you now hold. To Oprah, I extend my deepest gratitude, heartfelt thanks, and my sincerest well wishes.

The second person I want to recognise is Alain de Botton, the esteemed British philosopher who founded the School of Life. I have delved into their articles and perused their books, with one of my favourites being the one on good parenting. My continued engagement with their content and profound emphasis on emotional intelligence resonate deeply with me. In the modern era, the importance of emotional intelligence cannot be overstated, as it can be nurtured, honed, and enhanced. I am profoundly grateful for the wealth of resources provided by the School of Life. I even had the privilege of attending one of their workshops right here in Sydney, which was about discovering a career path that truly aligns with one's aspirations.

The third individual I wish to acknowledge is Jim Rohn, whose wisdom I have primarily encountered through his influential book *The Five Major Pieces to the Life Puzzle*. My journey as an avid reader commenced with this book, and the message that deeply resonated with me was his insight that humans tend to opt for the path of least resistance. In other words, it is often easier not to take action than to take action. This lesson has remained with me through the years, and I am profoundly thankful for this source of wisdom.

The fourth person I would like to express my gratitude to is James Clear. His book, *Atomic Habits*, has had a profound impact on my life, and I eagerly await his weekly newsletter, '1-2-3,' which never fails to provide nuggets of wisdom. His writing style, marked by clarity and simplicity, has a unique way of conveying complex ideas. While there are other notable books on habits, such as *The Power of Habit*, James Clear's work has been a valuable resource in my personal development journey, and for that, I am sincerely thankful.

I am also indebted to several remarkable individuals I have encountered through their podcasts, books, and impactful contributions to education, science, and thought leadership.

One such individual is Andrew Huberman, whose podcast, 'Huberman Lab,' has been a source of enlightenment. As a university professor in neuroscience, his mission to demystify science for the broader public resonates deeply with my values of education, awareness, and knowledge sharing. The diverse range of topics he explores and the calibre of guests he invites make his podcast a treasure trove of wisdom. I have learned a great deal from him and continue to do so with every episode.

Another luminary I would like to mention is Simon Sinek. His book, *Start with Why*, has been profoundly influential in my life. Simon's unique presentation style, marked by expressive facial mimics and gestures, conveys the potential of a great teacher and presenter. His work on purpose and leadership has left an indelible mark, and for that, I express my heartfelt gratitude.

A master of enlightening perspectives, Yuval Noah Harari, has fundamentally transformed my view of history, world religions, and human behaviour. I have devoured three of his books, including *Homo Sapiens, Homo Deus*, and *21 Lessons for the 21st Century*. His profound insights into the complexities of the twenty-first century are mind-blowing. His writing and reasoning have made him a profound influence and mentor in my life, and I am immensely grateful for his work.

I'd like to express my gratitude to another influential figure in my life, John Kehoe. John, a Canadian speaker and presenter, is renowned for his teachings on harnessing the power of the mind. I first encountered his work over a decade ago, if not more, and delved into his materials with great enthusiasm. While life took me on various paths, I found myself returning to his mind-power techniques time and again.

John's teachings, his distinctive speaking style, and the exercises he prescribes have been a wellspring of inspiration throughout my journey. His emphasis on persistence and his insights into human potential have left an indelible mark on my life. I am genuinely thankful for the serendipitous moment when I first stumbled upon his materials, and I deeply value the wisdom he imparts. Thank you, John, for your invaluable contributions to my personal growth.

Lastly, my journey of perseverance and resilience has been deeply enriched by reading accounts of Auschwitz survivors, Anne Frank's diary, and other Holocaust-related literature. These stories, filled with unimaginable human suffering and remarkable resilience, have been a beacon of strength for me. Titles like *Man's Search for Meaning* by Viktor E. Frankl, *The Diary of Anne* Frank, *The Tattooist of Auschwitz* by Heather Morris, and *The Choice* by Dr. Edith Eger have been both eye-opening and profoundly inspirational. They remind me of the extraordinary strength of the human spirit in the face of unimaginable adversity.

In their collective wisdom, these authors and thinkers have provided me with invaluable insights and perspectives, and I am forever grateful for their contributions to my personal and intellectual growth.

I would like to take a moment to express my profound gratitude to every person and every soul who has crossed my path at some point in my life, whether for a brief moment or an extended period. Each of you has left a mark on my journey, be it through positive inspiration or challenging lessons.

In every encounter, I have gained invaluable insights. Every interaction and every conversation have contributed to my growth, shaping the person I have become. I extend my deepest and most heartfelt appreciation to each and every individual who has shared a part of their life with me.

Thank you, for you have all played a unique role in my life experiences.

Oprah Winfrey

Oprah Winfrey—an icon of resilience, determination, and boundless success. My journey into the world of Oprah began during my high school years, within the pages of an English reading book. Her story, a tapestry of hardship, perseverance, and triumph, left an indelible mark on my soul. The inspiration I drew from her experiences would guide me through the different phases of my life.

As a student, our reading material was carefully curated, sometimes censored. However, I yearned to learn more about Oprah. Over time, my connection with this remarkable woman deepened. I delved into her 21-day meditation challenges led by the renowned Deepak Chopra. Hearing her voice, experiencing her wisdom, was nothing short of mesmerising. I devoured her shows, savoured her words, and read her book. An unshakeable dream had taken root within me: I aspired to stand alongside Oprah, to work with her, to share my own journey, my 'yellow labelled' book. This dream was etched into the fabric of my being, a long-held desire that I nurtured and visualised, often seeing myself seated across from Oprah in one of her famous interviews.

My book is not just a story; it is a testament to courage and resilience. It is the narrative of my choice to leave Iran, my birthplace, and embark on a new life in Australia as a PhD student on a scholarship. Armed with nothing but two suitcases, this journey was a Herculean feat. The book recounts two years of relentless scholarship applications because, without them, I lacked the financial means to study abroad. Beyond the financial constraints, there was another hurdle: convincing my family to let go of a long-standing marriage. My departure had been announced, and it was clear to me that the key to both freedom and growth lay in education. In a household where education was revered, I was no exception. My parents were teachers, as was my brother, and I had followed in their footsteps. I was a teacher. However, the path ahead was far from certain.

I applied to universities in various countries, but scholarships were highly competitive. Then, one Monday morning in May in 2015, an email arrived, bearing miraculous news—I had been awarded a scholarship to leave both my marriage and Iran. The path ahead was clear, even if the journey would be long and arduous. It was a realisation I cherished: I was not a tree, bound to a specific patch of soil. I had the power to choose a different life, a life I could mould according to my own vision.

And so, my dreams of Oprah continued to bloom. I envisioned our meeting, in a glamorous setting with lush greenery as the backdrop, a place where we would sit, talk, and share stories. Oprah, holding my yellow-covered book, would tell me how inspiring it was, not just for girls in Iran but for people all around the world. This vision, this burning desire, became an integral part of my being. I could feel the forces of the universe rallying behind my dream, conspiring to make it a reality.

I had stepped out of my comfort zone long ago, challenging myself to reach out to someone as famous and celebrated as Oprah. It was an audacious endeavour, and although I received no response, my message was not in vain. I had sent it to the universe, and I knew that one day, the moment I had envisioned, the interview in the midst of nature's lush embrace, would materialise. I was ready for the day Oprah and I would sit together, surrounded by the beauty of nature, holding my book, engaged in a conversation that would inspire countless others.

This dream is close. So close, I can almost touch it.

Affirmations

Affirmations are more than just words; they are resounding affirmatives, encapsulating your essence in bold letters. They serve as a profound reminder that you are exceptional, deserving, loved, and resilient. As you commit to positive and productive affirmations, they evolve beyond mere statements—they become the core beliefs shaping your values and ultimately defining who you are. These affirmations, when infused with emotion and vigour, breathe life into your journey of self-transformation.

In recognition of their significance, I present a list of affirmations that have been a source of strength and motivation in my own life. I prefer to keep them simple and concise, allowing me to repeat them effortlessly in various situations—stuck in traffic, battling negative thoughts, facing moments of uncertainty, or seeking a boost of motivation. Feel free to adopt and adapt these affirmations to resonate with different aspects of your life, employing them as a powerful tool in your on-going transformation.

Let these affirmations echo within you, transforming not just your thoughts but also your habits, and ultimately, your entire being.

A List of Affirmations

- I am great.
- I deserve all the best.
- I love myself.
- I respect myself.
- I am worth it.
- I am stronger than I think.
- I am invincible.
- I am an amazing human being.
- I have oceanic potential.
- I believe in myself.
- I see great things in my future.
- I am creative.
- I am as light as a feather.
- I am fit.
- I am healthy.
- I am strong.
- I vibrate with positive energy.
- My life is full of abundance.
- I am born for success.
- I feel successful.
- I have tons of energy.
- I make the best decisions.
- I am on the path to greatness.
- I choose wisely.
- I am a healthy eater.
- I love doing exercise.
- I go positive; I go first.
- I love my life.
- I am surrounded by awesome friends.
- I have the best job.

- I love my job.
- I am disciplined.
- I attract only greatness.
- I am positive.
- I am productive.
- I shine my light.
- I am kind.
- I am compassionate.
- I am a respected citizen.
- I think big.
- I trust myself.
- I am lucky.
- I love my family.
- I am safe.
- I am loved.
- I am loving.
- I am supported.
- The universe supports me.
- I feel fabulous.
- I am invested in success.
- I am invested in myself.
- I am determined.
- I am hopeful.
- All is fantabulous.
- I am grateful.
- My life is filled with love.
- I am the light.
- I share my light.
- Mother Nature supports me.
- I am assertive.
- I am confident.

- I am athletic.
- I am consistent.
- I always get results.
- I am calm and relaxed.
- I trust the timing of the universe.
- I am committed.
- I am empathetic.
- I value myself.
- I am valuable.
- I am useful.
- I am conscientious.
- I know the art of living.
- I cultivate mind power.
- I choose my thoughts wisely.
- I am wise.
- I am aware.
- I am conscious.
- I am courageous.
- I am dedicated.
- I create my life.
- I am my life's director.
- I am unique.
- My success benefits everyone.
- I acknowledge my success.
- I enjoy life.
- I have fun every day.
- I see the positive in every situation.
- I am audacious.
- I am benevolent.
- I am caring.
- I excel in job interviews.

- People love me.
- I invest in myself.
- I am an avid reader.
- I have a clear purpose.
- I am my best friend.
- I shine my light.
- I am a quick learner.
- I am mindful.
- I have peace of mind.
- I am blessed.
- I have all I need now.
- I am present.
- I am energised.
- I am pumped.